OLD MOORE'S

HOROSCOPE
AND ASTRAL
DIARY

•

TAURUS

foulsham
LONDON • NEW YORK • TORONTO • SYDNEY

foulsham
Yeovil Road, Slough, Berkshire, SL1 4JH

ISBN 0-572-01906-8

Printed in: Great Britain at
Cox & Wyman Ltd, Reading

CONTENTS

OLD MOORE'S HOROSCOPE AND ASTRAL DIARY

Old Moore's Horoscope and Astral Diary represents a major departure from the usual format of publications dedicated to popular Sun-sign astrology. In this book, more attention than ever before has been focused on the discovery of the 'real you', through a wealth of astrological information, presented in an easy to follow and interesting form, and designed to provide a comprehensive insight into your fundamental nature.

The interplay of the Sun and Moon form complex cycles that are brought to bear on each of us in different ways. In the pages that follow I will explain how a knowledge of these patterns in your life can make relationships with others easier and general success more possible. Realising when your mind and body are at their most active or inactive, and at what times your greatest efforts are liable to see you winning through, can be of tremendous importance. In addition, your interaction with other zodiac types is explored, together with a comprehensive explanation of your Sun-sign nature,

In the Astral Diary you will discover a day-to-day reading covering a fifteen-month period. The readings are compiled from solar, lunar and planetary relationships as they bear upon your own zodiac sign. In addition, easy-to-follow graphic charts offer you at a glance an understanding of the way that your personal life-cycles are running; what days are best for maximum effort and when your system is likely to be regenerating.

Because some people want to look deeper into the fascinating world of personal astrology, there is a section of the book allowing a more in-depth appraisal of the all-important zodiac sign that was 'Rising' at the time of your birth. You can also look at your own personal 'Moon Sign' using simple to follow instructions to locate the position of this very significant heavenly body on the day that you were born.

From a simple-to-follow diary section, on to an intimate understanding of the ever-changing child of the solar system that you are, my Horoscope and Astral Diary will allow you to unlock potential that you never even suspected you had.

With the help and guidance of the following pages, Old Moore wishes you a happy and prosperous future.

HERE'S LOOKING AT YOU

A ZODIAC PORTRAIT OF TAURUS
(21st APRIL - 21st MAY)

The typical misrepresentation of Taurus is that of a thick-set Bull-like character, with bulbous protruding eyes and a short neck. In fact, nothing could be further from the truth since, ruled as they are by Venus, Taureans tend to be amongst the best looking people in the zodiac. Even amongst the most ordinary of these individuals there is something inherently attractive. The tendency is towards dark hair and eyes, though the complexion is light and clear and the skin is particularly fine. The whole impression is one of fullness, with a squarish face, full mouth and lips, a strong purposeful jaw and well sculpted features.

Taurus possesses the best speaking voice of any sign, since the throat and the vocal chords are under the rulership of the Bull. Although not especially witty or entertaining speakers, Taureans are simply pleasant to listen to, with a harmonious quality that lifts any oration. Taurus produces good singers, actors and professional speakers of all types. Of course, there are two sides to every coin and this region of the body is the one that is inclined to give problems if life style is ignored.

Venus is the natural ruler of the sign of Taurus, a certain indicator of the natural sense of harmony, beauty and refinement the Bull accepts as being second nature. The Taurean home is inclined to be light and airy, full of pastel shades and reflecting the great outdoors, which is the natural home of all these bovine counterparts.

In terms of general health, the Taurean is inclined to be fairly robust, a little too much so if some care is not exercised when it comes to diet. It is a sad fact of all people ruled by Venus that an early, natural beauty of form can be turned into a parrody of poise and elegance by a life of over-eating and a failure to keep generally fit and in trim. Chronic disorders are few here and the nervous system, though often misused, does tend to be fairly strong. This is aided by the Bull's refusal to be rushed or forced into anything.

THE INTENTION

The word tangible is defined as perceptible by touch, and what drives Taurus on is the need to experience the heights and depths of physical reality. This is achieved via the favourite channels of the sign; acquisition of money and possessions, a love of food and drink and general sensuality. It is fair to say that as an Earth sign, Taurus is rooted in the realms of the materialistic most of the time, its desire being to give form to the surrounding energies in the universe, to make things permanent and secure. This makes Taureans interested in tangible realities, rather than the creative energy that precedes them. Because of this it is not unusual to find the Bull participating in forms of art that result in a three-dimensional representation of subject matter, as is the case with sculpture. Taureans also make fine mechanical engineers, and, because of their natural country rulership, are often to be found working on farms or in market gardens. The Bull is attracted to nature in all its forms, another legacy of the Earth element, and also the love of beauty inherent in the planet Venus.

Through the five physical senses the Taurean experiences the world at large and is often artistic enough to translate what it takes in, especially through the medium of fine-art, design, interior decorating, even through the kind of muscular creativity exemplified by the Blacksmith.

Taureans are generally attracted to religion in its most basic form, if at all, and can happily experience their version of God through the colours of a painting, the key changes in a symphony, the taste of freshly cooked fish and chips, or a beautifully formed human body. All is grist to the mill as far as the Bull is concerned.

YOUR VIRTUES

The more colourful facets of the Taurean personality are expressed through a warmth and friendliness that is genuine and sincere; and you, the observer, realises that you are dealing with someone who values the integrity of your personality. If you are a phoney however, Taurus will spot you a mile away. It cannot abide superficiality in anyone, or those pretending to be something that they are not. Mother Nature is a governing factor in the Bull's approach to life. Synthetic anything tends to be shunned, and healthy, fresh food in opposition to frozen or processed are invariably the option. The home of the Taurean is inclined to reflect a knowing elegance and it is true to say that the average discerning Taurean would choose one really good item of furniture in preference to a house filled with plywood.

The orientation towards quality in people is also evident. When Taurus is happy and secure with the position it occupies in the world at large, it would be difficult to envisage meeting a more gentle or charming individual. There is a steady dependability and an air of refinement within this personality, so that it is not at all hard to lean on the solidity under-pinning this earthiest of signs. You won't be let down if you do, Taurus enjoys a chat as much as anyone, but it is steadfast and loyal, willing to suffer torture sooner than to betray a confidence.

The Bull can be bold and fearless, and it may come as a surprise to realise that medals for bravery under fire are more likely to be won by a Taurean than by any other sign of the zodiac. The reason for this sems to lie in the Bull's loyalty to its friends and also in its temper. It takes great effort to annoy this character, though once you succeed - look out. Taurus fights willingly for its family or friends, knows no limits to strength or staying-power and can usually be relied on to come out on top. As far as success is concerned, dogged determination is the key to riches with this character.

YOUR VICES

Victorian astrologers invariably portrayed Taureans as having a bad memory, a basically hostile attitude (albeit masked by a quiet, unassuming manner) and very little imagination in the sphere of creative pursuits. All of this reflects the inherent bestiality of the bovine sign that the historical astrologers believed they could recognised. Fortunately this is far from the truth, which is not to suggest that the average Taurean belongs in the realms of the saints - far from it. Animal cunning might not be far from the mark, but the Bull has a very good memory, especially if owed money or in the throes of bearing a grudge. Taurus can wait to get even, and often does, though the Bull will only take so much baiting before it reacts instinctively and with great force. Either way, upset a Taurean just once and it could take you a long time to get back into their good books again.

A lack of imagination certainly does not appear to be the case when it comes to an appreciation of beauty in all its forms, though can become evident in the Taurean tendency to stick doggedly to what it understands and appreciates, be it a certain district to live in, or a particular television programme to watch. Taureans can be possessive, especially in relationships, over-careful with money, generally acquisitive and also brooding if upset or crossed.

LIVING A HAPPY LIFE

Seen from your own point of perspective, there is nothing especially complex about your nature. You take life pretty much in your stride and would be practical enough to get by, even if you found yourself living on the proverbial desert island. It is the world of realities that takes your fancy, with all its attendant sights, smells, flavours and other sensual experiences.

Taurus rules the throat and to some extent the chest. These are the areas that will give you the most problems if you try to do too much or push that cast iron constitution beyond sensible limits. Your diet should be wholesome and pure and you need plenty of rest, especially if you are called upon to exercise your mental faculties to any great extent.

There is little doubt that, when crossed, you can be one of the most stubborn individuals in the zodiac. Up against another Taurean you could find yourself struggling for years without ever reaching a satisfactory conclusion. Nevertheless, you are especially patient and will generally achieve your objectives by dint of perseverance and the drive to work long and hard.

Your relationships are usually secure and happy. You need a partner who is not so flighty that their movements become a blur to you, though one who is stimulating enough to offer some of the lightness of touch that your own nature can lack, especially if you find yourself living under pressure. Family is quite important and the Bull takes well to looking after children. You could be rather authoritarian in your approach to younger people and should try hard to remain young; it's far too easy for your sometimes heavy sign to get stuck in its ways and to indoctrinate your children with your own prejudices. Friends are not easily formed but will probably stick with you through thick and thin once they do come along.

WHAT'S RISING

YOUR RISING SIGN AND PERSONALITY

Perhaps you have come across this term 'Rising Sign' when look-ing at other books on astrology and may have been somewhat puzzled as to what it actually means. To those not accustomed to astrological jargon it could sound somewhat technical and mysterious, though in fact, in terms of your own personal birth chart, it couldn't be simpler. The Rising Sign is simply that part of the zodiac occupying the eastern horizon at the time of your birth. Because it is a little more difficult to discover than your sun-sign, many writers of popular astrology have tended to ignore it, which is a great shame, because, together with the Sun, your Rising Sign is the single most important factor in terms of setting your personality. So much so, that no appraisal of your astrological nature could be complete without it.

Your Rising Sign, also known as your 'Ascendant' or 'Ascen-ding Sign' plays a great part in your looks - yes, astrology can even predict what you are going to be like physically. In fact, this is a very interesting point, because there appears to be a tie-in between astrology and genetics. Professional Astrologers for centuries have noted the close relationship that often exists bet-ween the astrological birth chart of parents and those of their offspring, so that, if you look like your Mother or Father, chances are that there is a close astrological tie-up. Rising signs especial-ly appear to be handed down through families.

The first impression that you get, in an astrological sense, upon meeting a stranger, is not related to their sun-sign but to the zodiac sign that was rising at the moment they came into the world. The Rising Sign is particularly important because it modifies the way that you display your Sun-sign to the world at large. A good example of this might be that of Britain's best-known ex- Prime minister, Margaret Thatcher. This dynamic and powerful lady is a Libran by Sun-sign placing, indicating a light-hearted nature, pleasure loving and very flexible. However, Mrs Thatcher has Scorpio as her Rising Sign, bringing a steely determination and a tremendous capacity for work. It also bestows an iron will and the power to thrive under pressure.

Here lies the true importance of the Rising Sign, for Mr Thatcher almost certainly knows a woman who most other people do not. The Rising Sign is a protective shell, and not until we know someone quite well do we start to discover the Sun-sign nature that hides within this often tough outer coat of astrological making. Your Rising Sign also represents your basic self-image, the social mask that is often so useful; and even if you don't think that you conform to the interpretation of your Ascendant, chances are that other people will think that you do.

The way that an individual looks, walks, sits and generally presents themselves to the world is all down to the Rising Sign. For example, a person possessed of Gemini Rising is apt to be very quick, energetic in all movements, deliberate in mannerisms and with a cheerful disposition. A bearer of a Taurean Ascendant on the other hand would probably not be so tall, more solid generally, quieter in aspect and calmer in movement. Once you come to understand the basics of astrology it is really very easy to pick out the Rising Signs of people that you come across, even though the Sun-sign is often more difficult to pin down. Keep an eye open for the dynamic and positive Aries Rising individual, or the retiring, shy but absolutely magnetic quality of of the Piscean Ascendant. Of course, in astrology, nothing is quite that simple. The position of a vast array of heavenly bodies at the time of birth also has to be taken into account, particularly that of the Moon and the inner planets Mercury and Venus. Nevertheless a knowledge of your Rising sign can be an invaluable aid in getting to know what really makes you tick as an individual.

To ascertain the exact degree of your Rising sign takes a little experience and recourse to some special material. However, I have evolved a series of tables that will enable you to discover at a glance what your Rising Sign is likely to be. All you need to know is the approximate time of your birth. At the back of the book you will find the necessary table related to your Sun-sign. Simply look down the left-hand column until you find your approximate time of birth, am or pm. Now scan across the top of the table to the place where your date of birth is shown. Look for the square where the two pieces of information connect and there is your Rising Sign. Now that you know what your Rising Sign is, read on, and learn even more about the fascinating interplay of astrological relationship.

TAURUS WITH TAURUS RISING

As with all people who share the same Rising sign and Sun sign, you would be considered by the world at large to be very typical of your part of the zodiac. Kind and understanding, you can on occasions also be very stubborn, especially if you are crossed over something that you see to be of particular importance. Once you have made your mind up to something, there is no force in the world strong enough to distract you or cause you to wander from your chosen path.

Taureans are usually creative and are lovers of beauty. This is doubly true in your case, so it is very important that you are able to create the sort of surroundings that you find to be comfortable and harmonious. You can toil long and hard to achieve your objectives and generally win through in the end. It is possible that you will occasionally be accused of lacking imagination, mainly because you know what you like and tend to stick to it. You make a good friend and a faithful partner.

TAURUS WITH GEMINI RISING

Here the slow, plodding, methodical Bull takes a back seat, in favour of the get-up-and-go quality of the Twins; at least that is how it is likely to appear to the world at large. Sensitive types may consider that there is something about you that just doesn't ring true, because they are picking up on the very real reserve that underpins that gregarious exterior. Only those that know you very well would be fully in tune with your occasional silences.

You like to think of yourself as being logically minded, rational and methodical, even though you often wander off into the netherworld of dreams and intuitions. The combination is rather a strange one, not least of all because the quieter Taurean is liable to be swamped by Gemini, making it difficult for the two qualities to be reconciled harmoniously. The Gemini side of your nature is always wanting to be at the forefront of things, and especially to be communicating, and yet you are enough of a Bull to keep your counsel over issues that you do not feel qualified to comment upon. It's all a little confusing, not least of all for you, making for a life that can be rather difficult on occasions. In your lighter moments however you can enjoy the best of both worlds.

TAURUS WITH CANCER RISING

You make a great fuss of your friends, perhaps because deep inside you have the feeling that they belong to you. Certainly you have enduring relationships that tend to last a lifetime, and you can be guaranteed to offer a warm welcome, congenial chat and a warm fire whenever pals turn up. Looking after others is the Cancerian way, amplified in this case by the presence of Taurus, which has an overriding need to maintain the status quo. Be careful that you don'y stifle, when in reality you merely seek to nurture. Not everyone wants to have their life organised in the way that you find so instinctive.

You can be fairly reserved when faced with people who you don't know all that well, being quite shy and vulnerable to slights. However, outsiders seldom penetrate the tough exterior that represents both the hide of the Bull and the shell of the Crab, and it is from within the realms of your own intimates that hurts can be generated. The most important emphasis of all is on security. In a quiet and unassuming way your life is filled with successes.

TAURUS WITH LEO RISING

Far be it from me to accuse anyone of almost total self love, but let us face it, you do come quite close. That dignified Leonine exterior is certain to get you noticed. This is not a problem, in fact you actively seek the attention that so naturally comes your way. Nevertheless you are generous, warm-hearted and very brave. There is great power within your nature to do almost anything that you turn your mind to, you have courage, fortitude and endurance..

What you really need is a greater insight into the fact that not everyone in the world at large thinks about things in quite the same way that you do. Sometimes you show a distinct lack of patience with those individuals who dare to contradict your point of view and despite your generous and noble spirit, you can be a little obsessive about being in the right. You have a very strong desire nature, inclining you towards some jealousy and possessiveness, though you are loyal, protective and loving, particularly when you feel that it is your duty to take a particular individual under your wing. Getting some enjoyment from your life could be a problem sometimes.

13

TAURUS WITH VIRGO RISING

With this double Earth sign combination you typify your Sun sign of Taurus in most respects. Thus within you is evident all the conservative, level-headed qualities of the Bull. On top of this however there is great adaptability, which, it might might be argued is the one thing that Taureans tend to lack. You are quite able to bend with the wind of change, and can achieve singly greater success in most areas of your life as a result. Communication is possible through the influence of Mercury-ruled Virgo, even though no Earth sign person could be considered to be from the most chatty area of the zodiac.

There is a tendency for you to see things in purely black and white terms, insisting that there is a rational explanation for almost everything. This is a belief that you can administer with a nit picking persistence, often to the annoyance of more flexible types. Everything in its place is certainly your motto and woe betide the people who have the courage to disagree. For all this you are loving, and free with advice and practical help.

TAURUS WITH LIBRA RISING

Libra sits comfortably with almost any sign, though few more harmoniously than that of Taurus. You graduated from the charm school of life at a very early age. With the most subtle of persuasion you manage to acquire all the things that the Taurean within you desires and other people seem grateful that they have had the chance to assist you on your way. You are a natural diplomat and peace-maker, filled with Venusian charm and able to turn most circumstances round to your own advantage.

The presence of Libra means that you are not as earthy as the typical Taurean would be, and this means that there is significantly more flexibility within your nature. Look for interests that involve you with others, work in a complaints department and you may even have people apologising to you that they have bought your shoddy goods. Your conversation can be shallow on occasions, but never dull, meaning that you are the life and soul of any party that you choose to attend. Watch out for a slightly greedy streak, especially where food is concerned.

TAURUS WITH SCORPIO RISING

This can be a rather heavy combination, with a fixed and often inflexible attitude that allows little in the way of compromise once you have made your mind up to any particular course of action. In short, you know what you like and what you want, so that it takes considerable effort on the part of others to find any degree of flexibility within you. On the reverse side, you are absolutely loyal, would stick to your friends through thick and thin and are unlikely to let the little idiosyncrasies of others prevent you from backing them up.

With Taurus and Scorpio together, there is a double dose of sensuality, and the emphasis for you is on the pleasures generated by, and owing to, the five senses. This means that you are fond of food and drink, home comforts and probably sex. You don't over- intellectualise any situation but are never-the-less a very deep thinker. Passions are reserved for those people who share your very private world, those who can look deep inside that complex, brooding nature.

TAURUS WITH SAGITTARIUS RISING

This represents an interesting combination since your broad-minded and optimistic Sagittarian persona masks a rather parochial, somewhat stick-in-the-mud individual. Your Rising sign runs quite contrary to the intentions and desires of Taurus, so there is bound to be a degree of disparity within your nature. On some occasions the bright, warm and diffuse qualities of the Archer will predominate, so that you are good to have around, though there is a much quieter side to your personality too and an inherent need for solitude on occasions.

Security is always going to be important to you in one way or another, together with the need for firm roots. At the same time you love to be entertaining and also to know what makes the whole world tick. At times you are inclined to over-spend, a situation that, as in so many other things, creates conflict between the opposing qualities of your nature. When out and about in the world you do like to look and feel good and on those occasions when you may have had one glass of wine more than is really good for you, it is possible to observe the Archer making a bid for freedom. You don't really like to upset others but find this to be inevitable on occasions.

TAURUS WITH CAPICORN RISING

Locked up in the practical world as you are, other less materialistic souls might find you rather dull and uninspiring on occasions. This is a feeling inspired by the sometimes sober and conservative image that you present. You can be sensitive to this, and the fact itself can lead to a sort of self-conscious striving and too much of a desire to be interesting.

Life is generally a serious business for you, though you are happiest when in control and in the company of people that you have come to know and trust. You have good managerial ability and are usually successful in a career sense. On a more personal level, you need the company of someone who looks at life in a more light-hearted way and can be greatly influenced for the good if your own rather darker nature is subjected to a fun-filled atmosphere for any length of time. To this end you may choose to associate with either Geminis or Sagittarians, both signs that would take you right out of yourself and find, below the surface, the fun-loving individual you can really be.

TAURUS WITH AQUARIUS RISING

With your ability to analyse anything and everything, you would make a really good scientist, in fact many of you probably already are. High-flying theories and philosophies; religious tracts or mystical parables are all grist to the mill of your active and constantly ruminating mind. Things have to make sense to you, though it is a sense that conforms to your own particular rational world view.

Aquarius Rising is often accused of being rather eccentric, even weird on occasions, not that you are especially bothered what other people are inclined to call you. You are happiest in social settings, where you always have something original and interesting to say. Your life-style is fairly normal, which may surprise others a little, though the people closest to you are aware that you can even be a traditionalist when the mood takes you. You are both a thinker and a doer, so much so that your combination of signs is often attracted to the practical side of teaching, where your various skills could all find a sensible means of expression. You will certainly never be short of friends, even if one or two of them turn out to be every bit as unusual as you are.

TAURUS WITH PISCES RISING

Yours is a deeply passionate and caring nature. It is true that you often look at the world through rose-tinted spectacles, for you really do want everything in you life to be coated in glamour, beauty and pleasantness. Life doesn't always come up to your expectations for certain, but you make an excellent job of smoothing out the rough edges, not least of all with your optimism. Helping others is almost an integral part of your life and there are no lengths to which you would refuse to go in order to support someone for whom you really cared.

It is true that you can on occasions be something of a hedonist, happy to escape into a paradise of your senses (often including gluttony and sloth). Many people with this combination seek to find solace and comfort in stimulants of one sort or another, disguising their excesses from the world by overlaying them with a sense of respectability. Only learn to control such excesses and yours can be a contented life. A good, sound relationship could be vital.

TAURUS WITH ARIES RISING

In many respects you are a fairly typical Sun Taurus; how you differ lies mainly in your rather dynamic and spirited approach to life. There are occasions when your caution and reserve disappear altogether, as the placid Bull is transformed into the quick-tempered Ram. These sudden changes of character can come as a complete surprise to the people around you. You do possess Taurean thoroughness, which combined with the driving success coming from the direction of the Ram can make you a force to be reckoned with. In times of stress or difficulty you really come into your own and may well have been the type of person who could turn the course of a battle in former, more violent days.

Your approach to others could appear to be rather un-subtle and cavalier on occasions, though you mean no harm and can work tirelessly on behalf of the ones you love. Even if you are inclined to railroad your ideas, it does so often mean that at least something is getting done. In this respect you are a destroyer of red tape, which could make you one or two enemies on your way through life. The Aries side of your personality is inclined to opt for regular change.

TAURUS
IN LOVE AND FRIENDSHIP

WANT TO KNOW HOW WELL YOU GET ON WITH OTHER ZODIAC SIGNS?

THE TABLES BELOW DEAL WITH LOVE AND FRIENDSHIP

THE MORE HEARTS THERE ARE AGAINST ANY SIGN OF THE ZODIAC, THE BETTER THE CHANCE OF CUPID'S DART SCORING A DIRECT HIT.

THE SMILES OF FRIENDSHIP DISPLAY HOW WELL YOU WORK OR ASSOCIATE WITH ALL THE OTHER SIGNS OF THE ZODIAC.

Love					Sign	Friendship				
	♥	♥	♥	♥	**ARIES**	☺	☺	☺		
♥	♥	♥	♥	♥	**TAURUS**	☺	☺	☺	☺	
			♥	♥	**GEMINI**	☺	☺	☺		
			♥	♥	**CANCER**	☺	☺	☺		
		♥	♥	♥	**LEO**	☺	☺			
♥	♥	♥	♥	♥	**VIRGO**	☺	☺	☺	☺	☺
		♥	♥	♥	**LIBRA**	☺	☺			
			♥	♥	**SCORPIO**	☺	☺	☺		
		♥	♥	♥	**SAGITTARIUS**	☺	☺	☺	☺	
♥	♥	♥	♥	♥	**CAPRICORN**	☺	☺	☺	☺	☺
			♥	♥	**AQUARIUS**	☺	☺	☺		
		♥	♥	♥	**PISCES**	☺	☺			

THE MOON AND YOUR DAY-TO-DAY LIFE

Look up at the sky on cloudless nights and you are almost certain to see the Earth's closest neighbour in space, engaged in her intricate and complicated relationship with the planet upon which we live. The Moon isn't very large, in fact only a small fraction of the size of the Earth, but it is very close to us in spatial terms, and here lies the reason why the Moon probably has more of a part to play in your day-to-day life than any other body in space.

It is fair to say in astrological terms that if the Sun and Planets represent the hour and minute hands regulating your character swings and mood changes, the Moon is a rapidly sweeping second hand, governing emotions especially, but touching practically every aspect of your life.

Although the Moon moves so quickly, and maintains a staggeringly complex orbital relationship with the Earth, no book charting the possible ups and downs of your daily life could be complete without some reference to lunar action. For this reason I have included a number of the more important lunar cycles that you can observe within your own life, and also give you the opportunity to discover which zodiac sign the Moon occupied when you were born. Follow the instructions below and you will soon have a far better idea of where astrological cycles come from, and the part they play in your life.

SUN MOON CYCLES

The first lunar cycle deals with the relationship that the Moon keeps with your Sun sign. I have made the fluctuations of this pattern easy for you to understand by means of a simple cyclic graph. It appears on the first page of each 'Your Month At A Glance', under the title 'Highs and Lows'. The graph displays the lunar cycle and you will soon learn to understand how its movements have a bearing on your level of energy and your abilities. Once you recognise the patterns, you can work within them, making certain that your maximum efforts are expounded at the most opportune time.

MOON AGE CYCLES

Looking at the second lunar pattern that helps to make you feel the way you do, day-to-day, involves a small amount of work on your part to establish how you slot into the rhythm. However, since Moon Age cycles are one of the most potent astrological forces at work in your life, the effort is more than worthwhile.

This cycle refers to the way that the date of your birth fits into the Moon Phase pattern. Because of the complex relationship of the Earth and the Moon, we see the face of the lunar disc change throughout a period of roughly one month. The time between one New Moon (this is when there is no Moon to be seen) to the next New Moon, is about 29 days. Between the two the Moon would have seemed larger each night until the lunar disc was Full; it would then start to recede back towards New again. We call this cycle the Moon Age Cycle and classify the day of the New Moon as day 0. Full Moon occurs on day 15 with the last day of the cycle being either day 28 or day 29, dependent on the complicated motions of the combined Earth and Moon.

If you know on what Moon Age Day you were born, then you also know how you fit into the cycle. You would monitor the changes of the cycle as more or less tension in your body, an easy or a strained disposition, good or bad temper and so forth. In order to work out your Moon Age Day follow the steps below:

STEP 1: Look at the two New Moon Tables on pages 23 and 24. Down the left hand column you will see every year from 1902 to 1994 listed, and the months of the year appear across the top. Where the year of your birth and the month that you were born coincide, the figure shown indicates the date of the month on which New Moon occurred.

STEP 2: You need to pick the New Moon that occurred prior to your day of birth, so if your birthday falls at the beginning of the month, you may have to refer to the New Moon from the previous month. Once you have established the nearest New Moon prior to your birthday, (and of course in the correct year), all you have to do is count forward to your birthday. (Don't forget that the day of the New Moon is classed as 0.) As an example, if your were born on March 22nd 1962, the last New Moon before your birthday would have occurred on 6th March 1962. Counting forward from 6 to 22 would mean that you were born on Moon Age

Day 16. If your Moon Phase Cycle crosses the end of February, don't forget to check whether or not you were born in a Leap Year. If so you will have to compensate for that fact.

HOW TO USE MOON AGE DAYS

Once you know your Moon Age Day, you can refer to the Diary section of the book, because there, on each day of the year, you will see that the Moon Age Day is listed. The day in each cycle that conforms to your own Moon Age monthly birthday should find you in a positive and optimistic frame of mind Your emotions are likely to be settled and your thinking processes clear and concise. There are other important days that you will want to know about on this cycle, and to make matters simpler I have compiled an easy to follow table on pages 25 and 26. Quite soon you will get to know which Moon Age Days influence you, and how.

Of course Moon Age Cycles, although specific to your own date of birth, also run within the other astrological patterns that you will find described in this book. So, for example, if your Moon Age Day coincided with a particular day of the month, but everything else was working to the contrary, you might be wise to delay any particularly monumental effort until another, more generally favourable, day. Sometimes cycles run together and occasionally they do not; this is the essence of astrological prediction.

YOUR MOON SIGN

Once you have established on what Moon Age Day you were born, it isn't too difficult to also discover what zodiac sign the Moon occupied on the day of your birth. Although the Moon is very small in size compared to some of the solar system's larger bodies, it is very close indeed to the Earth and this seems to give it a special astrological significance. This is why there are many cycles and patterns associated with the Moon that have an important part to play in the lives of every living creature on the face of our planet, Of all the astrological patterns associated with the Moon that have a part to play in your life, none is more potent than those related to the zodiac position of the Moon at birth. Many of the most intimate details of your personal make-up are related to your Moon Sign, and we will look at these now.

HOW TO DISCOVER YOUR MOON SIGN

The Moon moves through each sign of the zodiac in only two to three days. It also has a rather complicated orbital relationship with the Earth; for these reasons it can be difficult to work out what your Zodiac Moon Sign is. However, having discovered your Moon Age Day you are half way towards finding your Moon Sign, and in order to do so, simply follow the steps below:

STEP 1: Make sure that you have a note of your date of birth and also your Moon Age Day.

STEP 2: Look at Zodiac Moon Sign Table 1 on page 27. Find the month of your birth across the top of the table, and your date of birth down the left. Where the two converge you will see a letter. Make a note of the letter that relates to you.

STEP 3: Now turn to Zodiac Moon Sign Table 2 on pages 28 and 30. Look for your Moon Age Day across the top of the tables and the letter that you have just discoverd down the left side. Where the two converge you will see a zodiac sign. The Moon occupied this zodiac sign on the day of your birth.

PLEASE NOTE: The Moon can change signs at any time of the day or night, and the signs listed in this book are generally applicable for 12 noon on each day. If you were born near the start or the end of a particular Zodiac Moon Sign, it is worth reading the character descriptions of adjacent signs. These are listed pages 30to 35. So much of your nature is governed by the Moon at the time of your birth that it should be fairly obvious wich one of the profiles relates to you.

YOUR ZODIAC MOON SIGN EXPLAINED

You will find a profile of all Zodiac Moon Signs on pages 30 to 35, showing in yet another way astrology helps to make you into the individual that you are. In each month in the Astral Diary, in addition to your Moon Age Day, you can also discover your Zodiac Moon Sign birthday (that day when the Moon occupies the same zodiac sign as it did when you were born). At these times you are in the best postion to be emotionally steady and to make the sort of decisions that have real, lasting value.

NEW MOON TABLE

YEAR	JAN	FEB	MAR	APR	MAY	JUN	JUL	AUG	SEP	OCT	NOV	DEC
1902	9	8	9	8	7	6	5	3	2	1/30	29	29
1903	27	26	28	27	26	25	24	22	21	20	19	18
1904	17	15	17	16	15	14	14	12	10	18	8	8
1905	6	5	5	4	3	2	2/31	30	28	28	26	26
1906	24	23	24	23	22	21	20	19	18	17	16	15
1907	14	12	14	12	11	10	9	8	7	6	5	5
1908	3	2	3	2	1/30	29	28	27	25	25	24	24
1909	22	20	21	20	19	17	17	15	14	14	13	12
1910	11	9	11	9	9	7	6	5	3	2	1	1/30
1911	29	28	30	28	28	26	25	24	22	21	20	20
1912	18	17	19	18	17	16	15	13	12	11	9	9
1913	7	6	7	6	5	4	3	2/31	30	29	28	27
1914	25	24	26	24	24	23	22	21	19	19	17	17
1915	15	14	15	13	13	12	11	10	9	8	7	6
1916	5	3	5	3	2	1/30	30	29	27	27	26	25
1917	24	22	23	22	20	19	18	17	15	15	14	13
1918	12	11	12	11	10	8	8	6	4	4	3	2
1919	1/31	-	2/31	30	29	27	27	25	23	23	22	21
1920	21	19	20	18	18	16	15	14	12	12	10	10
1921	9	8	9	8	7	6	5	3	2	1/30	29	29
1922	27	26	28	27	26	25	24	22	21	20	19	18
1923	17	15	17	16	15	14	14	12	10	10	8	8
1924	6	5	5	4	3	2	2/31	30	28	28	26	26
1925	24	23	24	23	22	21	20	19	18	17	16	15
1926	14	12	14	12	11	10	9	8	7	6	5	5
1927	3	2	3	2	1/30	29	28	27	25	25	24	24
1928	21	19	21	20	19	18	17	16	14	14	12	12
1929	11	9	11	9	9	7	6	5	3	2	1	1/30
1930	29	28	30	28	28	26	25	24	22	20	20	19
1931	18	17	19	18	17	16	15	13	12	11	9	9
1932	7	6	7	6	5	4	3	2/31	30	29	2	27
1933	25	24	26	24	24	23	22	21	19	19	17	17
1934	15	14	15	13	13	12	11	10	9	8	7	6
1935	5	3	5	3	2	1/30	30	29	27	27	26	25
1936	24	22	23	21	20	19	18	17	15	15	14	13
1937	12	11	12	12	10	8	8	6	4	4	3	2
1938	1/31	-	2/31	30	29	27	27	25	23	23	22	21
1939	20	19	20	19	19	17	16	15	13	12	11	10
1940	9	8	9	7	7	6	5	4	2	1/30	29	28
1941	27	26	27	26	26	24	24	22	21	20	19	18
1942	16	15	16	15	15	13	13	12	10	10	8	8
1943	6	4	6	4	4	2	2	1/30	29	29	27	27
1944	25	24	24	22	22	20	20	18	17	17	15	15
1945	14	12	14	12	11	10	9	8	6	6	4	4
1946	3	2	3	2	1/30	29	28	26	25	24	23	23
1947	21	19	21	20	19	18	17	16	14	14	12	12

NEW MOON TABLE

YEAR	JAN	FEB	MAR	APR	MAY	JUN	JUL	AUG	SEP	OCT	NOV	DEC
1948	11	9	11	9	9	7	6	5	3	2	1	1/30
1949	29	27	29	28	27	26	25	24	23	21	20	19
1950	18	16	18	17	17	15	15	13	12	11	9	9
1951	7	6	7	6	6	4	4	2	1	1/30	29	28
1952	26	25	25	24	23	22	23	20	29	28	27	27
1953	15	14	15	13	13	11	11	9	8	8	6	6
1954	5	3	5	3	2	1/30	29	28	27	26	25	25
1955	24	22	24	22	21	20	19	17	16	15	14	14
1956	13	11	12	11	10	8	8	6	4	4	2	2
1957	1/30	-	1/31	29	29	27	27	25	23	23	21	21
1958	19	18	20	19	18	17	16	15	13	12	11	10
1959	9	7	9	8	7	6	6	4	3	2/31	30	29
1960	27	26	27	26	26	24	24	22	21	20	19	18
1961	16	15	16	15	14	13	12	11	10	9	8	7
1962	6	5	6	5	4	2	1/31	30	28	28	27	26
1963	25	23	25	23	23	21	20	19	17	17	15	15
1964	14	13	14	12	11	10	9	7	6	5	4	4
1965	3	1	2	1	1/30	29	28	26	25	24	22	22
1966	21	19	21	20	19	18	17	16	14	14	12	12
1967	10	9	10	9	8	7	7	5	4	3	2	1/30
1968	29	28	29	28	27	26	25	24	23	22	21	20
1969	1 9	17	18	16	15	14	13	12	11	10	9	9
1970	7	6	7	6	6	4	4	2	1	1/30	29	28
1971	26	25	26	25	24	22	22	20	19	19	18	17
1972	15	14	15	13	13	11	11	9	8	8	6	6
1973	5	4	5	3	2	1/30	29	28	27	26	25	25
1974	24	22	24	22	21	20	19	17	16	15	14	14
1975	12	11	12	11	11	9	9	7	5	5	3	3
1976	1/31	29	30	29	29	27	27	25	23	23	21	21
1977	19	18	19	18	18	16	16	14	13	12	11	10
1978	9	7	9	7	7	5	5	4	2	2/31	30	29
1979	27	26	27	26	26	24	24	22	21	20	19	18
1980	16	15	16	15	14	13	12	11	10	9	8	7
1981	6	4	6	4	4	2	1/31	29	28	27	26	26
1982	25	23	24	23	21	21	20	19	17	17	15	15
1983	14	13	14	13	12	11	10	8	7	6	4	4
1984	3	1	2	1	1/30	29	28	26	25	24	22	22
1985	21	19	21	20	19	18	17	16	14	14	12	12
1986	10	9	10	9	8	7	7	5	4	3	2	1/30
1987	29	28	29	28	27	26	25	24	23	22	21	20
1988	19	17	18	16	15	14	13	12	11	10	9	9
1989	7	6	7	6	5	3	3	1/31	29	29	28	28
1990	26	25	26	25	24	22	22	20	19	18	17	17
1991	15	14	15	13	13	11	11	9	8	8	6	6
1992	4	3	4	3	2	1/30	29	28	26	25	24	24
1993	24	22	24	22	21	20	19	17	16	15	14	14
1994	11	10	12	11	10	9	8	7	5	5	3	2

MOON AGE QUICK REFERENCE TABLE

SIGNIFICANT MOON AGE DAYS

		+ Days	- Days	* Days
Y	0	4, 6, 12, 14, 19, 21, 25, 28	9, 16, 23	0
O	1	5, 7, 13, 15, 20, 22, 26, 29	10, 17, 24	1
U	2	0, 6, 8, 14, 16, 21, 23, 27	11, 18, 25	2
R	3	1, 7, 9, 15, 17, 22, 24, 28	12, 19, 26	3
	4	2, 8, 10, 16, 18, 23, 25, 29	13, 20, 27	4
O	5	0, 3, 4, 9, 11, 17, 19, 24, 26	14, 21, 28	5
W	6	1, 4, 5, 10, 12, 18, 20, 25, 27	15, 22, 29	6
N	7	2, 5, 11, 13, 19, 21, 26, 28	0, 16, 23	7
	8	3, 6, 12, 14, 20, 22, 27, 29	1, 17, 24	8
M	9	0, 4, 7, 13, 15, 21, 23, 28	2, 18, 25	9
O	10	1, 5, 8, 14, 16, 22, 24, 29	3, 19, 26	10
O	11	0, 2, 6, 9, 15, 17, 23, 25	4, 20, 27	11
N	12	1, 3, 7, 10, 16, 18, 24, 26	5, 21, 28	12
	13	2, 4, 8, 11, 17, 19, 25, 27	6, 22, 29	13
A	14	3, 5, 9, 12, 18, 20, 26, 28	0, 7, 23	14
G	15	4, 6, 10, 13, 19, 21, 27, 29	1, 8, 24	15
E	16	0, 5, 7, 11, 14, 20, 22, 28	2, 9, 25	16
	17	1, 6, 8, 12, 15, 21, 23, 29	3, 10, 26	17
D	18	0, 2, 7, 9, 13, 16, 22, 24	4, 11, 27	18
A	19	1, 3, 8, 10, 14, 17, 23, 25	5, 12, 28	19
Y	20	2, 4, 9, 11, 15, 18, 24, 26	6, 13, 29	20
	21	3, 5, 10, 12, 16, 19, 25, 27	0, 7, 14	21
	22	4, 6, 11, 13, 17, 20, 26, 28	1, 8, 15	22
	23	5, 7, 12, 14, 18, 21, 27, 29	2, 9, 16	23
	24	0, 6, 8, 13, 15, 19, 22, 28	3, 10, 17	24
	25	1, 7, 9, 14, 16, 20, 23, 29	4, 11, 18	25
	26	0, 2, 8, 10, 15, 17, 21, 24,	5, 12, 19	26
	27	1, 3, 9, 11, 16, 18, 22, 25	6, 13, 20	27
	28	2, 4, 10, 12, 17, 19, 23, 26	7, 14, 21	28
	29	3, 5, 11, 13, 18, 20, 24, 27	8, 15, 22	29

MOON AGE QUICK REFERENCE TABLE

The table opposite will allow you to plot the significant days on the Moon Age Day Cycle and to monitor the way they have a bearing on your own life. You will find an explanation of the Moon Age Cycles on pages 20 - 22. Once you know your own Moon Age Day, you can find it in the left-hand column of the table opposite, To the right of your Moon Age Day you will observe a series of numbers; these appear under three headings. + Days, - Days and * Days.

If you look at the Diary section of the book, immediately to the right of each day and date, the Moon Age Day number is listed. The Quick Reference Table allows you to register which Moon Age Days are significant to you. For example: if your own Moon Age Day is 5, each month you should put a + in the Diary section against Moon Age Days 0, 3, 4, 9, 11, 17, 19, 24, and 26. Jot down a - against Moon Age Days 14, 21 and 28, and a * against Moon Age Day 5. You can now follow your own personal Moon Age Cycle every day of the year.

+ Days are periods when the Moon Age Cycle is in tune with your own Moon Age Day. At this time life should be more harmonious and your emotions are likely to be running smoothly. These are good days for making decisions.

- Days find the Moon Age Cycle out of harmony with your own Moon Age Day. Avoid taking chances at these times and take life reasonably steady. Confrontation would not make sense.

* Days occur only once each Moon Age Cycle, and represent your own Moon Age Day. Such times should be excellent for taking the odd chance and for moving positively towards your objectives in life. On those rare occasions where a * day coincides with your lunar high, you would really be looking at an exceptional period and could afford to be quite bold and adventurous in your approach to life.

MOON ZODIAC SIGN TABLE 1

	Month	Jan	Feb	Mar	Apr	May	Jun	Jul	Aug	Sep	Oct	Nov	Dec
	1	A	D	F	J	M	O	R	U	X	a	e	i
	2	A	D	G	J	M	P	R	U	X	a	e	i
	3	A	D	G	J	M	P	S	V	X	a	e	m
	4	A	D	G	J	M	P	S	V	Y	b	f	m
	5	A	D	G	J	M	P	S	V	Y	b	f	n
	6	A	D	G	J	M	P	S	V	Y	b	f	n
	7	A	D	G	J	M	P	S	V	Y	b	f	n
	8	A	D	G	J	M	P	S	V	Y	b	f	n
D	9	A	D	G	J	M	P	S	V	Y	b	f	n
A	10	A	E	G	J	M	P	S	V	Y	b	f	n
Y	11	B	E	G	K	M	P	S	V	Y	b	f	n
	12	B	E	H	K	N	Q	S	V	Y	b	f	n
O	13	B	E	H	K	N	Q	T	V	Y	b	g	n
F	14	B	E	H	K	N	Q	T	W	Z	d	g	n
	15	B	E	H	K	N	Q	T	W	Z	d	g	n
M	16	B	E	H	K	N	Q	T	W	Z	d	g	n
O	17	B	E	H	K	N	Q	T	W	Z	d	g	n
N	18	B	E	H	K	N	Q	T	W	Z	d	g	n
T	19	B	E	H	K	N	Q	T	W	Z	d	g	n
H	20	B	F	H	K	N	Q	T	W	Z	d	g	n
	21	C	F	H	L	N	Q	T	W	Z	d	g	n
	22	C	F	I	L	O	R	T	W	Z	d	g	n
	23	C	F	I	L	O	R	T	W	Z	d	i	q
	24	C	F	I	L	O	R	U	X	a	e	i	q
	25	C	F	I	L	O	R	U	X	a	e	i	q
	26	C	F	I	L	O	R	U	X	a	e	i	q
	27	C	F	I	L	O	R	U	X	a	e	i	q
	28	C	F	I	L	O	R	U	X	a	e	i	q
	29	C	-	I	L	O	R	U	X	a	e	i	q
	30	C	-	I	L	O	R	U	X	a	e	i	q
	31	D	–	I	-	O	-	U	X	-	e	-	q

Moon Age Day	0	1	2	3	4	5	6	7	8	9	10	11	12	13
A	Ca	Aq	Aq	Aq	Pi	Pi	Ar	Ar	Ar	Ta	Ta	Ge	Ge	Ge
B	Aq	Aq	Aq	Pi	Pi	Ar	Ar	Ar	Ta	Ta	Ge	Ge	Ge	Cn
C	Aq	Aq	Pi	Pi	Ar	Ar	Ar	Ta	Ta	Ge	Ge	Ge	Cn	Cn
D	Aq	Pi	Pi	Pi	Ar	Ar	Ta	Ta	Ta	Ge	Ge	Cn	Cn	Le
E	Pi	Pi	Pi	Ar	Ar	Ta	Ta	Ta	Ge	Ge	Cn	Cn	Cn	Le
F	Pi	Pi	Ar	Ar	Ar	Ta	Ta	Ge	Ge	Cn	Cn	Cn	Le	Le
G	Pi	Ar	Ar	Ar	Ta	Ta	Ge	Ge	Ge	Cn	Cn	Le	Le	Le
H	Ar	Ar	Ar	Ta	Ta	Ge	Ge	Ge	Cn	Cn	Le	Le	Le	Vi
I	Ar	Ar	Ta	Ta	Ge	Ge	Ge	Cn	Cn	Cn	Le	Le	Vi	Vi
J	Ar	Ta	Ta	Ta	Ge	Ge	Cn	Cn	Cn	Le	Le	Vi	Vi	Vi
K	Ta	Ta	Ta	Ge	Ge	Cn	Cn	Cn	Le	Le	Vi	Vi	Vi	Li
L	Ta	Ta	Ge	Ge	Ge	Cn	Cn	Le	Le	Vi	Vi	Vi	Li	Li
M	Ta	Ge	Ge	Ge	Cn	Cn	Le	Le	Le	Vi	Vi	Li	Li	Li
N	Ge	Ge	Ge	Cn	Cn	Le	Le	Le	Vi	Vi	Li	Li	Li	Sc
O	Ge	Ge	Cn	Cn	Cn	Le	Le	Vi	Vi	Li	Li	Sc	Sc	Sc
P	Ge	Cn	Cn	Cn	Le	Le	Vi	Vi	Vi	Li	Li	Sc	Sc	Sc
Q	Cn	Cn	Cn	Le	Le	Vi	Vi	Li	Li	Sc	Sc	Sc	Sa	Sa
R	Cn	Cn	Le	Le	Le	Vi	Vi	Li	Li	Li	Sc	Sc	Sa	Sa
S	Cn	Le	Le	Le	Vi	Vi	Li	Li	Li	Sc	Sc	Sa	Sa	Sa
T	Le	Le	Le	Vi	Vi	Li	Li	Li	Sc	Sc	Sa	Sa	Sa	Ca
U	Le	Le	Vi	Vi	Li	Li	Li	Sc	Sc	Sa	Sa	Ca	Ca	Ca
V	Le	Vi	Vi	Vi	Li	Li	Sc	Sc	Sc	Sa	Sa	Ca	Ca	Ca
W	Le	Vi	Vi	Li	Li	Sc	Sc	Sa	Sa	Sa	Ca	Ca	Aq	Aq
X	Vi	Vi	Li	Li	Li	Sc	Sc	Sa	Sa	Sa	Ca	Ca	Aq	Aq
Y	Vi	Li	Li	Li	Sc	Sc	Sa	Sa	Sa	Ca	Ca	Aq	Aq	Aq
Z	Li	Li	Li	Sc	Sc	Sc	Sa	Sa	Ca	Ca	Ca	Aq	Aq	Pi
a	Li	Li	Li	Sc	Sc	Sa	Sa	Sa	Ca	Ca	Aq	Aq	Pi	Pi
b	Li	Li	Sc	Sc	Sa	Sa	Ca	Ca	Ca	Aq	Aq	Pi	Pi	Ar
d	Li	Sc	Sc	Se	Sa	Sa	Ca	Ca	Ca	Aq	Aq	Pi	Pi	Pi
e	Sc	Sc	Sc	Sa	Sa	Ca	Ca	Aq	Aq	Aq	Pi	Pi	Ar	Ar
f	Sc	Sc	Sa	Sa	Ca	Ca	Aq	Aq	Pi	Pi	Ar	Ar	Ta	Ta
g	Sc	Sa	Sa	Ca	Ca	Aq	Aq	Pi	Pi	Pi	Ar	Ar	Ta	Ta
i	Sa	Sa	Ca	Ca	Ca	Aq	Aq	Pi	Pi	Ar	Ar	Ta	Ta	Ge
m	Sa	Sa	Ca	Ca	Aq	Aq	Aq	Pi	Pi	Ar	Ar	Ta	Ta	Ge
n	Sa	Ca	Ca	Aq	Aq	Pi	Pi	Ar	Ar	Ta	Ta	Ta	Ge	Ge
q	Ca	Ca	Aq	Aq	Pi	Pi	Ar	Ar	Ar	Ta	Ta	Ge	Ge	Ge

LETTER

Ar = Aries Ta = Taurus Ge = Gemini Cn = Cancer Le = Leo
Aq = Aquarius

28

SIGN TABLE 2

14	15	16	17	18	19	20	21	22	23	24	25	26	27	28	29
Cn	Cn	Le	Le	Le	Vi	Vi	Li	Li	Li	Sc	Sc	Sa	Sa	Sa	Ca
Cn	Le	Le	Le	Vi	Vi	Li	Li	Li	Sc	Sc	Sa	Sa	Sa	Ca	Ca
Le	Le	Le	Vi	Vi	Vi	Li	Li	Sc	Sc	Sc	Sa	Sa	Ca	Ca	Ca
Le	Le	Vi	Vi	Vi	Li	Li	Sc	Sc	Sc	Sa	Sa	Ca	Ca	Aq	Aq
Le	Vi	Vi	Vi	Li	Li	Sc	Sc	Sc	Sa	Sa	Ca	Ca	Aq	Aq	Aq
Vi	Vi	Vi	Li	Li	Li	Sc	Sc	Sa	Sa	Sa	Ca	Ca	Aq	Aq	Aq
Vi	Vi	Li	Li	Li	Sc	Sc	Sa	Sa	Sa	Ca	Ca	Aq	Aq	Aq	Pi
Vi	Li	Li	Li	Sc	Sc	Sa	Sa	Sa	Ca	Ca	Aq	Aq	Aq	Pi	Pi
Li	Li	Li	Sc	Sc	Sc	Sa	Sa	Ca	Ca	Ca	Aq	Aq	Pi	Pi	Pi
Li	Li	Sc	Sc	Sc	Sa	Sa	Ca	Ca	Ca	Aq	Aq	Pi	Pi	Pi	Ar
Li	Sc	Sc	Sc	Sa	Sa	Ca	Ca	Ca	Aq	Aq	Pi	Pi	Pi	Ar	Ar
Li	Sc	Sc	Sa	Sa	Sa	Ca	Ca	Aq	Aq	Aq	Pi	Pi	Ar	Ar	Ar
Sc	Sc	Sa	Sa	Sa	Ca	Ca	Aq	Aq	Aq	Pi	Pi	Ar	Ar	Ar	Ta
Sc	Sa	Sa	Sa	Ca	Ca	Aq	Aq	Aq	Pi	Pi	Ar	Ar	Ar	Ta	Ta
Sa	Sa	Sa	Ca	Ca	Ca	Aq	Aq	Pi	Pi	Pi	Ar	Ar	Ta	Ta	Ta
Sa	Sa	Ca	Ca	Ca	Aq	Aq	Pi	Pi	Pi	Ar	Ar	Ta	Ta	Ta	Ge
Sa	Ca	Ca	Ca	Aq	Aq	Pi	Pi	Pi	Ar	Ar	Ta	Ta	Ta	Ge	Ge
Sa	Ca	Ca	Aq	Aq	Aq	Pi	Pi	Ar	Ar	Ar	Ta	Ta	Ge	Ge	Ge
Ca	Ca	Aq	Aq	Aq	Pi	Pi	Ar	Ar	Ar	Ta	Ta	Ge	Ge	Ge	Cn
Ca	Aq	Aq	Aq	Pi	Pi	Ar	Ar	Ar	Ta	Ta	Ge	Ge	Ge	Cn	Cn
Aq	Aq	Aq	Pi	Pi	Pi	Ar	Ar	Ta	Ta	Ta	Ge	Ge	Cn	Cn	Cn
Aq	Aq	Pi	Pi	Pi	Ar	Ar	Ta	Ta	Ta	Ge	Ge	Cn	Cn	Cn	Le
Pi	Pi	Pi	Pi	Ar	Ar	Ta	Ta	Ta	Ge	Ge	Cn	Cn	Cn	Le	Le
Pi	Pi	Pi	Ar	Ar	Ar	Ta	Ta	Ge	Ge	Ge	Cn	Cn	Le	Le	Le
Pi	Pi	Ar	Ar	Ar	Ta	Ta	Ge	Ge	Ge	Cn	Cn	Le	Le	Le	Vi
Pi	Pi	Ar	Ar	Ar	Ta	Ta	Ge	Ge	Ge	Cn	Cn	Le	Le	Le	Vi
Ar	Ar	Ar	Ar	Ta	Ta	Ge	Ge	Ge	Cn	Cn	Cn	Le	Le	Vi	Vi
Ar	Ar	Ar	Ta	Ta	Ta	Ge	Ge	Cn	Cn	Cn	Le	Le	Vi	Vi	Vi
Ar	Ar	Ta	Ta	Ge	Ge	Ge	Cn	Cn	Cn	Le	Le	Vi	Vi	Vi	Li
Ta	Ta	Ta	Ge	Ge	Ge	Cn	Cn	Cn	Le	Le	Le	Vi	Vi	Li	Li
Ge	Ta	Ge	Ge	Ge	Cn	Cn	Cn	Le	Le	Le	Vi	Vi	Li	Li	Li
Ge	Ta	Ge	Ge	Cn	Cn	Cn	Le	Le	Le	Vi	Vi	Li	Li	Li	Sc
Ge	Ge	Ge	Cn	Cn	Cn	Le	Le	Vi	Vi	Vi	Li	Li	Sc	Sc	Sc
Ge	Ge	Cn	Cn	Cn	Le	Le	Le	Vi	Vi	Vi	Li	Li	Sc	Sc	Sa
Cn	Ge	Cn	Cn	Le	Le	Le	Vi	Vi	Vi	Li	Li	Sc	Sc	Sc	Sa
Cn	Cn	Cn	Le	Le	Le	Vi	Vi	Li	Li	Li	Sc	Sc	Sa	Sa	Sa

Vi = Virgo Li = Libra Sc = Scorpio Sa = Sagittarius Ca = Capricorn
Pi = Pisces

MOON SIGNS

MOON IN ARIES

You have a strong imagination and a desire to do things in your own way. Showing no lack of courage you can forge your own path through life with great determination.

Originality is one of your most important attributes, you are seldom stuck for an idea though your mind is very changeable and more attention might be given over to one job at once. Few have the ability to order you around and you can be quite quick tempered. A calm and relaxed attitude is difficult for you to adopt but because you put tremendous pressure on your nervous system it is vitally important for you to forget about the cut and thrust of life from time to time. It would be fair to say that you rarely get the rest that you both need and deserve and becaue of this there is a chance that your health could break down from time to time.

Emotionally speaking you can be a bit of a mess if you don't talk to the folks that you are closest to and work out how you really feel about things. Once you discover that there are people willing to help you there is suddenly less necessity for trying to tackle everything yourself.

MOON IN TAURUS

The Moon in Taurus at the time you were born gives you a courteous and friendly manner that is likely to assure you of many friends.

The good things in life mean a great deal to you for Taurus is an Earth sign and delights in experiences that please the senses. This probably makes you a lover of good food and drink and might also mean that you have to spend time on the bathroom scales balancing the delight of a healthy appetite with that of looking good which is equally important to you.

Emotionally you are fairly stable and once you have opted for a set of standards you are inclined to stick to them because Taurus is a Fixed sign and doesn't respond particularly well to change. Intuition also plays an important part in your life.

MOON IN GEMINI

The Moon in the sign of Gemini gives a warm-hearted character, full of sympathy and usually ready to help those in difficulty. In some matters you are very reserved, whilst at other
times you are articulate and chatty: this is part of the paradox
of Gemini which always brings duplicity to the nature. The
knowledge you possess of local and national affairs is very
good, this strengthens and enlivens your intellect making you
good company and endowing you with many friends. Most of
the people with whom you mix have a high opinion of you and
will stand ready to leap to your defence, not that this is
generally necessary for although you are not martial by nature,
you are more than capable of defending yourself verbally.

Travel plays an important part in your life and the naturally inquisitive quality of your mind allows you to benefit greatly
from changes in scenery. The more you mix with people from
different cultures and backgrounds the greater your interest in
life becomes and intellectual stimulus is the meat and drink of
the Gemini individual.

You can gain through reading and writing as well as the cul-
tivation of artistic pursuits but you do need plenty of rest in
order to avoid fatigue.

MOON IN CANCER

Moon in Cancer at the time of birth is a most fortunate position
since the sign of Cancer is the Moon's natural home. This
means that the qualities of compassion and understanding
given by the Moon are especially enhanced in your nature and
you cope quite well with emotional pressures that would bother
others. You are friendly and sociably inclined. Domestic tasks
don't really bother you and your greatest love is likely to be for
home and family. Your surroundings are particularly important and you hate squalor and filth.

Your basic character, although at times changeable like the
Moon itself, depends upon symmetry. Little wonder then that
you are almost certain to have a love of music and poetry. Not
surprising either that you do all within your power to make
your surroundings comfortable and harmonious, not only for
yourself, but on behalf of the folk who mean so much to you.

MOON IN LEO

You are especially ambitious and self-confident. The best qualities of both the Moon and the Sign of Leo come together here to ensure that you are warm-hearted and fair, characteristics that are almost certain to show through no matter what other planetary positions your chart contains.

You certainly don't lack the ability to organise, either yourself or those around you, and you invariably rise to a position of responsibility no matter what you decide to do with your life. Perhaps it is just as well because you don't enjoy being an 'also ran' and would much rather be an important part of a small organisation than a menial in a larger one.

In love you are likely to be lucky and happy provided that you put in that extra bit of effort and you can be relied upon to build comfortable home surroundings for yourself and also those for whom you feel a particular responsibility. It is likely that you will have a love of pleasure and sport and perhaps a fondness for music and literature. Life brings you many rewards, though most of them are as a direct result of the effort that you are able to put in on your own behalf. All the same you are inclined to be more lucky than average and will usually make the best of any given circumstance.

MOON IN VIRGO

This position of the Moon endows you with good mental abilities and a keen receptive memory. By nature you are probably quite reserved, nevertheless you have many friends, especially of the opposite sex, and you gain a great deal as a result of these associations. Marital relationships need to be discussed carefully and kept as harmonious as possible because personal attachments can be something of a problem to you if sufficient attention is not given to the way you handle them.

You are not ostentatious or pretentious, two characteristics that are sure to improve your popularity. Talented and persevering you possess artistic qualities and are a good homemaker. Earning your honours through genuine merit you can work long and hard towards your objectives but probably show very little pride in your genuine achievements. Many short journeys will be undertaken in your life.

MOON IN LIBRA

With the Moon in Libra you have a popular nature and don't find it particularly difficult to make friends. Most folk like you, probably more than you think, and all get-together's would be more fun with you present. Libra, for all its good points, is not the most stable of astrological signs and as a result your emotions can prove to be a little unstable too. Although the Moon in Libra is generally said to be good for love and marriage, the position of the Sun, and also the Rising Sign, in your own birth chart will have a greater than usual bearing on your emotional and loving qualities.

You cannot live your life in isolation and must rely on other people, who are likely to play an important part in your decision making. Cooperation is crucial for you because Libra represents the 'balance' of life that can only be achieved through harmonious relationships. An offshoot of this fact is that you do not enjoy being disliked and, like all Librans are friendly to practically everybody.

Conformity is not always easy for you, because Libra is an Air sign and likes to go its own way.

MOON IN SCORPIO

Some people might call you a little pushy, in fact all you really want to do is live your life to the full, and to protect yourself and your family from the pressures of life that you recognise all too readily. You should avoid giving the impression of being sarcastic or too impulsive, at the same time using your energies wisely and in a constructive manner.

Nobody could doubt your courage which is great, and you invariably achieve what you set out to do, by force of personality as well as by the effort that you are able to put in. You are fond of mystery and are probably quite perceptive as to the outcome of situations and events.

Problems can arise in your relationships with members of the opposite sex, so before you commit yourself emotionally it is very important to examine your motives carefully and ensure that the little demon, jealousy, always a problem with Scorpio positions, does not cloud your judgement in love matches. You need to travel and can make gains as a result.

MOON IN SAGITTARIUS

The Moon is Sagittarius helps to make you a generous individual with humanitarian qualities and a kind heart. Restlessness may be an endemic part of your character for your mind is seldom still. Perhaps because of this you have an overwhelming need for change that could lead you to several major moves during your adult life. You are probably a reasonably sporting sort of person and not afraid to stand your ground on the occasions when you know that you are correct in your judgement. What you have to say goes right to the heart of the matter and your intuition is very good.

At work you are quick and efficient in whatever you choose to do, and because you are versatile you make an ideal employee. Ideally you need work that is intellectually demanding because you are no drudge and would not enjoy tedious routines. In relationships you anger quickly if faced with stupidity or deception, though you are just as quick to forgive and forget. Emotionally there are times when you allow your heart to rule your head.

MOON IN CAPRICORN

Born with the Moon in Capricorn, you are popular and may come into the public eye in one way or another. Your administrative ability is good and you are a capable worker. The watery Moon is not entirely at home in the Earth sign of Capricorn and as a result difficulties can be experienced, especially in the early years of life. Some initial lack of creative ability and indecision has to be overcome before the true qualities of patience and perseverance inherent in Capricorn can show through.

If caution is exercised in financial affairs you can accumulate wealth with the passing of time but you will always have to be careful about forming any partnerships because you are open to deception more than most. Under such circumstances you would be well-advised to gain professional advice before committing yourself. Many people with the Moon in Capricorn take a healthy interest in social or welfare work. The organisational skills that you have, together with a genuine sympathy for others, means that you are suited to this kind of career.

MOON IN AQUARIUS

With the Moon in Aquarius you are an active and agreeable person with a friendly easy going sort of nature. Being sympathetic to the needs of other people you flourish best in an easy going atmosphere. You are broad-minded, just, and open to suggestion, though as with all faces of Aquarius the Moon here brings an unconventional quality that not everyone would find easy to understand.

You have a liking for anything strange and curious as well a fascination for old articles and places. Journeys to such locations would suit you doubly because you love to travel and can gain a great deal from the trips that you make. Political, scientific and educational work might all be of interest to you and you would gain from a career in some new and exciting branch of science or technology.

Money-wise, you make gains through innovation as much as by concentration and it isn't unusual to find lunar Aquarians tackling more than one job at the same time. In love you are honest and kind.

MOON IN PISCES

This position assures you of a kind sympathetic nature, somewhat retiring at times but always taking account of others and doing your best to help them. As with all planets in Pisces there is bound to be some misfortune on the way through life. In particular relationships of a personal nature can be problematic and often through no real fault of your own. Inevitably though suffering brings a better understanding, both of yourself and of the world around you. With a fondness for travel you appreciate beauty and harmony wherever you encounter them and hate disorder and strife.

You are probably very fond of literature and could make a good writer or speaker yourself. The imagination that you possess can be readily translated into creativity and you might come across as an incurable romantic. Being naturally receptive your intuition is strong, in many cases verging on a mediumistic quality that sets you apart from the world. You might not be rich in hard cash terms and yet the gifts that you possess and display, when used properly, are worth more than gold.

THE ASTRAL DIARY

How the diagrams work

Through the *picture diagrams* in the Astral Diary I want to help you to plot your year. With them you can see where the positive and negative aspects will be found each month. To make the most of them all you have to do is remember where and when!

Let me show you how they work . . .

THE MONTH AT A GLANCE

Just as there are twelve separate Zodiac Signs, so Astrologers believe that each sign has twelve separate aspects to life. Each of the twelve segments relates to a different personal aspect. I number and list them all every month as a key so that their meanings are always clear.

The twelve major aspects of your life

Symbols above the box means 'positive'

Shading inside the box means 'ordinary'

Symbol below the box means 'negative'

I have designed this chart to show you how and when these twelve different aspects are being influenced throughout the year. When the number rests comfortably in its shaded box, nothing out of the ordinary is to be expected. However, when a box turns white, then you should expect influences to become active in this area of your life. Where the influence is positive I have raised a smiling sun above its number. Where it is a negative, I hang a little rain cloud beneath it.

YOUR ENERGY RHYTHM CHART

On the opposite page is a picture diagram in which I am linking your zodiac group to the rhythm of the moon. In doing this I have calculated when you will be gaining strength from its influence and equally when you may be weakened by it.

If you think of yourself as being like the tides of the ocean then you may understand how your own energies must rise and fall too. And if you understand how it works and when it is working, then you can better organise your activities to achieve more and get things done more easily.

YOUR ENERGY-RHYTHM CHART

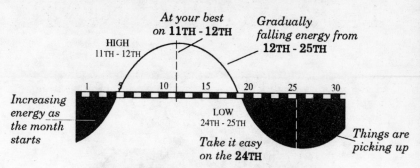

At your best on **11TH - 12TH**

Gradually falling energy from **12TH - 25TH**

HIGH 11TH - 12TH

Increasing energy as the month starts

LOW 24TH - 25TH

Take it easy on the **24TH**

Things are picking up

MOVING PICTURE SCREEN
Measured every week
LOVE, LUCK, MONEY & VITALITY

I hope that the diagram below offers more than a little fun. It is very easy to use. The bars move across the scale to give you some idea of the strength of opportunities open to you in each of the four areas. If LOVE stands at plus 4, then get out and put yourself about, because in terms of romance, things should be going your way. When the bar moves backwards then the opportunities are weakening and when it enters the negative scale, then romance should not be at the top of your list.

Not a good week for money

← NEGATIVE TREND

-5 -4 -3 -2 -1

POSITIVE TREND →

+1 +2 +3 +4 +5

Love at +4 promises a romantic week

Below average for vitality

| LOVE |
| MONEY |
| LUCK |
| VITALITY |

And your luck in general is good

And Finally:

am ....

pm ....

The two lines that are left blank in each daily entry of the Astral Diary are for your own personal use. You may find them ideal for keeping a check on birthdays or appointments, though it could be an idea to make notes from the astrological trends and diagrams a few weeks in advance. Some of the lines carry a key, as above. These days are important because they indicate the working of 'astrological cycles' in your life. The 'key' readings show how best you can act, react or simply work within them for greater success.

1993

YOUR MONTH AT A GLANCE

The twelve numbered boxes represent the important areas in your life.
The key to the numbers you will find beneath the panel. A Sun above
the number indicates that opportunities are around. A Cloud below
the number, that you should be a bit defensive. Nothing above or
below and life will be pretty ordinary.

☼				☼		☼					
1	2	3	4	5	6	7	8	9	10	11	12
	☁										

KEY

1 Strength of Personality
2 Personal Finance
3 Useful Information Gathering
4 Domestic Affairs
5 Pleasure & Romance
6 Effective Work & Health

7 One to One Relationships
8 Questioning, Thinking & Deciding
9 External Influences / Education
10 Career Aspirations
11 Teamwork Activities
12 Unconscious Impulses

OCTOBER HIGHS AND LOWS

Here, I show how the rhythm of the Moon will affect you this month.
Like the tide, your energies and abilities will rise and fall with its pattern. When it is above the date line, go-for-it. When it is below the
line you should be resting.

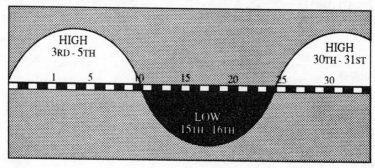

4 MONDAY
Moon Age Day 18 • Moon Sign Taurus

am ....

pm ....

It's full steam ahead for professional arrangements and for letting other people know how you feel about any subject under the sun. General good luck should be a hallmark of this period, and you can afford the odd flutter, as long as you know the risks involved, because even the Moon can't bring in rank outsiders every time.

5 TUESDAY
Moon Age Day 19 • Moon Sign Taurus

am ....

pm ....

Today could mark a make or break time for a particular relationship or a scheme that has been in the offing for a while now. Whatever happens, there should be no looking back and a refusal to use today's minor disappointments as a reason for modifying your efforts for the future. Be open minded.

6 WEDNESDAY
Moon Age Day 20 • Moon Sign Gemini

am ....

pm ....

The gentle breeze of change blows around you for a few days to come, allowing you the opportunity to look at situations again and to come to terms with the reasons for certain alterations to your life that you didn't choose personally. You should be left with the impression that most events really do turn out for the best in the end.

7 THURSDAY
Moon Age Day 21 • Moon Sign Gemini

am ....

pm ....

Even though you think you have been too busy or occupied with your own life to be of much use to others, you might begin to realise that you have been a tremendous help recently and can continue to be so now. This is just as important in a working sense as it is within the confines of your own family circle.

40

8 FRIDAY
Moon Age Day 22 • Moon Sign Cancer

am ....

pm ....

Matters associated with communication are highlighted, and should put you in a good mood one way or another. You will almost certainly be happy to see the end of the working week, mainly because you feel that your practical qualities have overpowered your desire to experience much in the way of fun recently.

9 SATURDAY
Moon Age Day 23 • Moon Sign Cancer

am ....

pm ....

Although you feel yourself to be firmly in the driving seat as far as your professional life is concerned, there are other people and situations to bear in mind. At the same time you are trying to conduct a difficult balancing act between work and home. If you simply calm down, you should be able to manage everything.

10 SUNDAY
Moon Age Day 24 • Moon Sign Leo

am ....

pm ....

A conflict of needs strikes home now. On the one hand you want to fulfil your responsibilities to the people that you care about the most, whilst at the same time recognising a part of yourself that needs quiet and isolation. What you probably feel is simply restlessness. Why not try something completely different?

← *NEGATIVE TREND*   *POSITIVE TREND* →

-5	-4	-3	-2	-1		+1	+2	+3	+4	+5
					LOVE					
					MONEY					
					LUCK					
					VITALITY					

11 MONDAY
Moon Age Day 25 • Moon Sign Leo

am ....

pm ....

With more confidence now and the courage of your convictions, especially in a professional sense, you can make much out of the present circumstances. There may still be a quiet place inside you that appears to be quite appealing, though to retreat into it now would certainly be a mistake.

12 TUESDAY
Moon Age Day 26 • Moon Sign Leo

am ....

pm ....

Positive planetary indicators now speak of a return to the more pleasure loving Taurean, with plenty to say and no shortage of people around to speak to. The solitary state won't seem half so appealing now and the need to co-operate will turn out to be of importance for its own sake, as well as a means of getting things done.

13 WEDNESDAY
Moon Age Day 27 • Moon Sign Virgo

am ....

pm ....

Presently in the midst of what should be an interesting, stimulating and even perhaps exciting time, you forget the meaning of the word can't and find yourself undertaking all sorts of tasks that you might have stayed clear of even just a couple of days ago. Loving relationships seem to grow ever stronger.

14 THURSDAY
Moon Age Day 28 • Moon Sign Virgo

am ....

pm ....

With duties and obligations once more to the forefront of your mind, some of the gilding is taken off your social life. Conversations could seem to be a little strained and even the most casual remarks passed by other people take on a double-edged significance. Try to control the pendulum mood swings that are a part of the present.

15 FRIDAY
Moon Age Day 0 • Moon Sign Libra

am ....

pm ....

There are decisions to be made before you can fully commit yourself to other people, or to situations that might be a bit difficult. Once you have finished with your thinking time, early in the day, personal horizons begin to widen and you should be on course for a generally straighter path. You need to feel in control.

16 SATURDAY
Moon Age Day 1 • Moon Sign Libra

am ....

pm ....

A weekend of sunny faces, when you can enjoy the last of 'the season of mists and mellow fruitfulness', could be just what the doctor ordered. Even casual conversations can fire off your enthusiasm and start your fertile mind thinking in radically different directions. Down in the mouth pals can easily be cheered up.

17 SUNDAY
Moon Age Day 2 • Moon Sign Scorpio

am ....

pm ....

The lunar low brings a more contemplative phase, though you have had your really quiet spell and won't want to retreat into yourself too much just at present. Look for a low-key interlude and enjoy the simple pleasures of home and family, or take a good look at the great outdoors before the winter begins to bite.

← *NEGATIVE TREND*   *POSITIVE TREND* →

-5	-4	-3	-2	-1		+1	+2	+3	+4	+5
					LOVE					
					MONEY					
					LUCK					
					VITALITY					

18 MONDAY
Moon Age Day 3 • Moon Sign Scorpio

am ....

pm ....

A fantastic link between the Sun and Jupiter blows some of the cob-webs of the lunar low away and allows you to review most situations in a new light. This should be the start of a high-point in your material life, where offers that mean a degree of advancement are more than likely and must be recognised for what they are.

19 TUESDAY
Moon Age Day 4 • Moon Sign Sagittarius

am ....

pm ....

Change, even to a fixed Taurean such as yourself, is the key to further success at present. Variety is certainly becoming the spice of your life and you should actively seek new possibilities, especially in a social sense. Many of the decisions that you make now will have long-term ramifications.

20 WEDNESDAY
Moon Age Day 5 • Moon Sign Sagittarius

am ....

pm ....

Nobody would accuse you of being lazy at present, even though you might feel from a personal point of view that everything you do takes extra effort . With Venus in your solar sixth house at the moment, it is more or less inevitable that some of your determina-tion seems to be absent and only time will make things clearer.

21 THURSDAY
Moon Age Day 6 • Moon Sign Capricorn

am ....

pm ....

Far more satisfying, especially as far as the details of your life are concerned, this day demands much in the way of concentration, but gives back tenfold what you put in. Complete outstanding tasks before you start new ones and don't be surprised if people want to help you without being asked to volunteer.

22 FRIDAY
Moon Age Day 7 • Moon Sign Capricorn

am ....

pm ....

A time that is not without its distractions and challenges, especially where professional interests are concerned. Others begin to realise that you are not to be trifled with and treat you with a greater degree of respect than might have been the case previously. Even superiors will be careful in their dealings with you.

23 SATURDAY
Moon Age Day 8 • Moon Sign Aquarius

am ....

pm ....

The Sun sails into your solar seventh house at this time, tending to bring a slightly quieter but definitely smoother path for you to walk during the coming month or so. There is greater goodwill from all directions to help you along, and even people that have been especially obstructive in the past now may see life as you do.

24 SUNDAY
Moon Age Day 9 • Moon Sign Aquarius

am ....

pm ....

Officialdom may have become quite tiresome. Let's face it, miles of red tape don't exactly inspire you at the best of times, but prove especially irksome just at the moment. What you cannot alter you must endure, even though this doesn't mean that you have to either agree with it or conform any more than you have to.

← *NEGATIVE TREND*   *POSITIVE TREND* →

-5	-4	-3	-2	-1		+1	+2	+3	+4	+5
					LOVE					
					MONEY					
					LUCK					
					VITALITY					

25 MONDAY
Moon Age Day 10 • Moon Sign Pisces

am ....

pm ....

It could feel as if others are giving you the runaround. Perhaps this has a little to do with the way that your mind is working at present. If you think back for a day or two it ought to be possible to realise that your usual patience has been at a premium. Looked at in this light, situations take on a different aspect.

26 TUESDAY
Moon Age Day 11 • Moon Sign Pisces

am ....

pm ....

Seeking alternative company turns out to be a stimulating and worthwhile exercise because new faces certainly bring out the best in you. Not surprising really. Everyone needs change in their life at some stage and you do stick to a favoured routine much more than most people do in any case.

27 WEDNESDAY
Moon Age Day 12 • Moon Sign Pisces

am ....

pm ....

Things generally will be developing as planned. So much so that there is probably little to do except to sit back and watch the show. You are unlikely to be in an argumentative frame of mind and would be unwilling to be drawn into one, even if you are provoked. All the same, stick to your point of view.

28 THURSDAY
Moon Age Day 13 • Moon Sign Aries

am ....

pm ....

Feeling yourself to be much more philosophical about your approach to life, the lengthy contact between Uranus and Neptune in Capricorn has helped you to take an overview recently, and that is why so many situations and relationships now seem to make much more sense to you.

29 FRIDAY

Moon Age Day 14 • Moon Sign Aries

am ....

pm ....

Slightly negative thoughts can be eradicated from your mind quickly, probably because it takes more to upset you on a Friday than it would at the beginning of the week. In any case, many people appear to be taking great delight in pleasing you, and in agreeing with what you have to say about most subjects.

30 SATURDAY

Moon Age Day 15 • Moon Sign Taurus

am ....

pm ....

A good way to finish any month is to discover that the lunar high pays our sign an additional visit. So it is for you right now, introducing a Saturday of some surprises and many laughs. You won't need too much encouragement to join in any fun and games that are taking place in our vicinity and worries are easily shelved.

31 SUNDAY

Moon Age Day 16 • Moon Sign Taurus

am ....

pm ....

Whereas you were inclined to push concern to the back of your mind yesterday, today you are more likely to take it out and dissect it. It is really amazing how worries become like mirages once you subject them to close scrutiny, and how much better you feel for having taken the trouble to do so.

← *NEGATIVE TREND* *POSITIVE TREND* →

-5	-4	-3	-2	-1		+1	+2	+3	+4	+5
					LOVE					
					MONEY					
					LUCK					
					VITALITY					

1993

YOUR MONTH AT A GLANCE

The twelve numbered boxes represent the important areas in your life. The key to the numbers you will find beneath the panel. A Sun above the number indicates that opportunities are around. A Cloud below the number, that you should be a bit defensive. Nothing above or below and life will be pretty ordinary.

☀							☀				☀
1	2	3	4	5	6	7	8	9	10	11	12
				☁							

KEY
1 Strength of Personality
2 Personal Finance
3 Useful Information Gathering
4 Domestic Affairs
5 Pleasure & Romance
6 Effective Work & Health

7 One to One Relationships
8 Questioning, Thinking & Deciding
9 External Influences / Education
10 Career Aspirations
11 Teamwork Activities
12 Unconscious Impulses

NOVEMBER HIGHS AND LOWS

Here, I show how the rhythm of the Moon will affect you this month. Like the tide, your energies and abilities will rise and fall with its pattern. When it is above the date line, go-for-it. When it is below the line you should be resting.

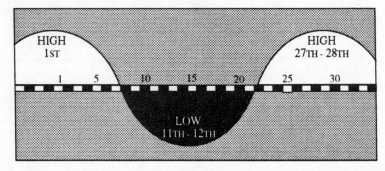

1 MONDAY
Moon Age Day 17 • Moon Sign Taurus

am ....

pm ....

There are some important issues about at present and they will need carefully handling during this working week. New incentives in out of work activities look like making the winter a time of great opportunity for those of you who are willing to join in. A shaky start to the month financially means nothing in he long-run.

2 TUESDAY
Moon Age Day 18 • Moon Sign Gemini

am ....

pm ....

You could have good reason to feel pleased with yourself concerning situations of the heart. Because you are seeing things so clearly now, personal attachments look like blossoming generally and even casual relationships could be taking on a new meaning. Friends should prove to be fairly trustworthy.

3 WEDNESDAY
Moon Age Day 19 • Moon Sign Gemini

am ....

pm ....

The financial prospects at present look as settled as they have for quite some time past, and because you have recently put so much effort into building a firmer foundation to your life, dividends begin to show any time now. The same is true in a relationship sense, though in this case you may have to work harder.

4 THURSDAY
Moon Age Day 20 • Moon Sign Cancer

am ....

pm ....

Issues on your social agenda seem to be time consuming, in all probability the arrangement of them is taking longer than the events you are planning. It could appear that your hours are so restricted that there are very few moments left for enjoyment and the secret is to make time for pleasure, no matter what.

5 FRIDAY

Moon Age Day 21 • Moon Sign Cancer

am ....

pm ....

Your powers of concentration and understanding are now both good, and that is one of the reasons that friends are turning to you for the impartial and sensible advice that you are inclined to offer. One-to-one relationships are less easy to fathom, being fine one day and often a little difficult on the next.

6 SATURDAY

Moon Age Day 22 • Moon Sign Cancer

am ....

pm ....

Personal happiness experienced this weekend might be partly dependent on how much work and worry you have brought home with you and the number of hours you are willing to spend coping with it. You really do need a rest from routines that are tedious at the best of times, even if you are busy in different ways.

7 SUNDAY

Moon Age Day 23 • Moon Sign Leo

am ....

pm ....

It is possible for you to restore harmony to family relationships and to tone down the demands of a few over-enthusiastic types, be they family members or just friends. Most of your efforts are being geared towards other people at present, which makes you someone that just about everyone would want to have around.

← *NEGATIVE TREND*   *POSITIVE TREND* →

-5	-4	-3	-2	-1		+1	+2	+3	+4	+5
					LOVE					
					MONEY					
					LUCK					
					VITALITY					

8 MONDAY
Moon Age Day 24 • Moon Sign Leo

am ....

pm ....

If you are uncertain about specific issues, especially those related to finance or work generally, there is no point at all in moving forward until you manage to clear your mind. Think things through and don't be afraid to consult other people before you proceed. Later in the week you will be pleased that you did.

9 TUESDAY
Moon Age Day 25 • Moon Sign Virgo

am ....

pm ....

Your ruling planet Venus now enters your solar seventh house and personal relationships take on a new significance for many of you. It's possible to feel much closer to your partner and also to certain individuals who were important to you in the past. Work may be somewhat eclipsed by personal possibilities.

10 WEDNESDAY
Moon Age Day 26 • Moon Sign Virgo

am ....

pm ....

Another favourable planetary movement occurs as Jupiter crosses into your solar seventh house of relationships and business arrangements. This is a long-term placement of Jupiter and means a year ahead when the balance between work and play is much easier to establish. Better luck could also be a factor.

11 THURSDAY
Moon Age Day 27 • Moon Sign Libra

am ....

pm ....

Completing an important trio of celestial happenings, Mars now has a part to play in your life. Bringing its positive influence to bear on your eighth house, you could find the deeper and more sensual pleasures of life forming a more important focus than would usually be the case. Don't go overboard though!

12 FRIDAY
Moon Age Day 28 • Moon Sign Libra

am ....

pm ....

Emotional considerations take centre stage for a while, as well as
the need to be feeding the more aesthetic aspects of your deeply creative nature. Even a stroll around an art gallery at lunch-time would
be of great benefit, or perhaps a peek in the decorating shop to plan
changes to your home that you want to implement later.

13 SATURDAY
Moon Age Day 0 • Moon Sign Scorpio

am ....

pm ....

The lunar low arriving in time for the weekend could turn out to
have distinct advantages. For one thing you won't be trying so hard
to do a dozen things at once, allowing a degree of flexibility for pleasing yourself. You might be in the mood for some shopping, but won't
be likely to find the best bargains under present circumstances.

14 SUNDAY
Moon Age Day 1 • Moon Sign Scorpio

am ....

pm ....

Your partner, or certain family members, may well be proving to be
far more capable in certain directions than you have given them
credit for in the past. One difficulty you might encounter would be
to rely on people born under the same sign as you are; a definite case
of the blind leading the blind, for today at least.

← NEGATIVE TREND								POSITIVE TREND →				
-5	-4	-3	-2	-1				+1	+2	+3	+4	+5
					LOVE							
					MONEY							
					LUCK							
					VITALITY							

15 MONDAY

Moon Age Day 2 • Moon Sign Sagittarius

am ....

pm ....

After the recent gains in your social and personal life come a series of challenges from officialdom, particularly people who do have a part to play in your search for more personal freedom. Red tape has rarely got your goat more than it does now and breaking free from it can be a tortuous business for many children of Venus at present.

16 TUESDAY

Moon Age Day 3 • Moon Sign Sagittarius

am ....

pm ....

Certain personal contacts are either being laid aside now, or are in need of a drastic re-thinking. There is a tendency for reliable and sensitive Taurus to cling to things, even if they have had their day and no longer serve any useful purpose. Avoid this restricting habit if at all possible and keep an eye on the future.

17 WEDNESDAY

Moon Age Day 4 • Moon Sign Capricorn

am ....

pm ....

The theme of transformation continues into today, though it should now be getting much easier to kiss goodbye to situations that really haven't done you any favours at all in the past. On the financial front you would be far better looking towards long-term gains than grabbing the money and running if some little incentive comes along.

18 THURSDAY

Moon Age Day 5 • Moon Sign Capricorn

am ....

pm ....

There could be a chance to secure your position and also to take part in some important decision making professionally. It doesn't matter if you are the Chairman of the Board or the person who paints the beaks on plastic ducks, relatively speaking, the degree of success that you can experience now is exactly the same for all of you.

19 FRIDAY

Moon Age Day 6 • Moon Sign Aquarius

am ....

pm ....

The spotlight is still apt to be on career and your thoughts for the future as far ahead as you can realistically see. Before the day is out you will be allowing your mind to dwell on more personal considerations, even if there is little to cloud our horizons in this sense. Tie up all the loose ends that you can.

20 SATURDAY

Moon Age Day 7 • Moon Sign Aquarius

am ....

pm ....

For some strange reason, the whole world and his dog seem to know what is best for you, and what is more don't give you the credit for knowing yourself at all. People mean well, so it might be best to bite your lip and say nothing. In the end all the decisions will be yours to take, no matter what the rest of the world says.

21 SUNDAY

Moon Age Day 8 • Moon Sign Aquarius

am ....

pm ....

A significant release of pressure is almost inevitable now, though the way it is expressed will differ from person to person. One thing that you could happily do without is a family row, and it would be far better to discover a deserted hill top and shout to the wind. The fresh air would do you good, as well as the release of tension.

← *NEGATIVE TREND*   *POSITIVE TREND* →

-5	-4	-3	-2	-1			+1	+2	+3	+4	+5
					LOVE						
					MONEY						
					LUCK						
					VITALITY						

22 MONDAY
Moon Age Day 9 • Moon Sign Pisces

am ....

pm ....

The Sun enters your solar eighth house now and the theme of
renewal becomes ever more important. It might be the wrong time
of year for spring cleaning, though that is effectively the process that
is taking place inside you right now. The clearer the decks - the
quicker you can hoist the sails and get yourself racing with the wind.

23 TUESDAY
Moon Age Day 10 • Moon Sign Pisces

am ....

pm ....

Personal relationships push forward on an emotional high. Contacts
with others, both general and specific, can only be of benefit to you
now and conteracts a tendency towards lethargy. Most of your conclusions are arived at as a result of sensible and positive thinking,
though don't forget the power of your intuition.

24 WEDNESDAY
Moon Age Day 11 • Moon Sign Aries

am ....

pm ....

It appears that nobody is frightened to let you know what they are
thinking right now and you may even be getting a little tired of so
much truth. Still, it's possible to lose yourself in the often routine
tasks that you have to undertake, and to mix with people of your
own choosing once your day's work is out of the way.

25 THURSDAY
Moon Age Day 12 • Moon Sign Aries

am ....

pm ....

It's time to dig deep into your own emotional depths, in order to discover how you really feel about the way other people are behaving,
especially in situations when their actions have a profound bearing
on your own life. You could be missing some important aspects of
your own subconscious thinking, so tune in for a few days..

26 FRIDAY

Moon Age Day 13 • Moon Sign Aries

am ....

pm ....

It won't be more than a matter of hours before the lunar low offers new incentives and tops up your somewhat depleted energy reserves. In the meantime, finish off the working week in the way that suits you the best. One thing you are unlikely to be doing is toiling as hard as you can right up until the last minute.

27 SATURDAY

Moon Age Day 14 • Moon Sign Taurus

am ....

pm ....

You have had to wait some time this month to feel the benefits that come from having the Moon is your own sign of Taurus. The advantage of such a happening at the weekend is that most of you will have the chance to really benefit from the situation. You won't have to look far for energy, it's there for the asking!

28 SUNDAY

Moon Age Day 15 • Moon Sign Taurus

am ....

pm ....

Some slight restlessness pays you a visit, which is a shame if the weather turns out to be awful and it isn't easy for you to get out of the house. All the same, you should make the effort, taking like minded people along with you if you can. Anything old, unusual or distinctly curious would no doubt take your fancy just at present.

← *NEGATIVE TREND*   *POSITIVE TREND* →

-5	-4	-3	-2	-1		+1	+2	+3	+4	+5
					LOVE					
					MONEY					
					LUCK					
					VITALITY					

29 MONDAY   *Moon Age Day 16 • Moon Sign Gemini*

am ....

pm ....

You find yourself on the receiving end of a powerful link between Venus and Pluto. Long standing arrangements become a dominant factor in your thinking for the next few days, though it is important that you do not allow colleagues to have greater power over your thought processes than you would personally wish.

30 TUESDAY   *Moon Age Day 17 • Moon Sign Gemini*

am ....

pm ....

You would do well to widen your horizons a little as the day wears on but don't take too much notice of the twists and turns of fate, especially when they don't have a bearing on your own destiny. Under all circumstances listen to the small voice inside you. It offers the best advice and knows you inside out.

1 WEDNESDAY   *Moon Age Day 18 • Moon Sign Gemini*

am ....

pm ....

You have had a very busy year and it might take you a while to realise that December is here already. You certainly won't be ready for thoughts about Christmas yet, even though people might be reminding you all the time of its proximity. What you are doing is pushing ahead rapidly with exciting new plans of your own.

2 THURSDAY   *Moon Age Day 19 • Moon Sign Cancer*

am ....

pm ....

Energy levels are high now and you will find that although the difficult is achieved easily, the impossible will take just a little longer. Other people might find it hard to keep up with your present lightening thought processes, so you may have to slow down from time to time, in order to let them catch up.

3 FRIDAY
Moon Age Day 20 • Moon Sign Cancer

am ....

pm ....

Look for help when you need it and count on the support of colleagues who are also personal friends. Although you might be trying
to keep social contacts to a minimum for the moment, there are some
important possibilities about just at present and it wouldn't help you
much to turn them down.

4 SATURDAY
Moon Age Day 21 • Moon Sign Leo

am ....

pm ....

Anything that depresses you should be left well alone now, even if
that means delaying jobs that have been outstanding for quite a
while. The best interludes come from arrangements that are made
at the last minute, and especially in the company of people who
mean a great deal to you. Some shopping might be fun!

5 SUNDAY
Moon Age Day 22 • Moon Sign Leo

am ....

pm ....

Get to grips with domestic necessities, though not to the exclusion of
your own personal needs, whatever they might be. It is all too easy
to jump to the wrong conclusions in a romantic sense and it might be
sensible to listen very closely to what other people have to say on the
subject before you react.

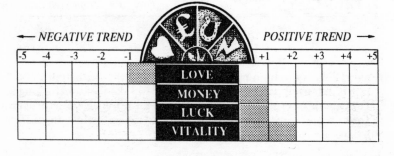

← NEGATIVE TREND							POSITIVE TREND →				
-5	-4	-3	-2	-1			+1	+2	+3	+4	+5
					LOVE						
					MONEY						
					LUCK						
					VITALITY						

1993

YOUR MONTH AT A GLANCE

The twelve numbered boxes represent the important areas in your life. The key to the numbers you will find beneath the panel. A Sun above the number indicates that opportunities are around. A Cloud below the number, that you should be a bit defensive. Nothing above or below and life will be pretty ordinary.

1	2	3	4	5	6	7	8	9	10	11	12

Suns above 5, 9 and 10. Cloud below 8.

KEY

1 Strength of Personality
2 Personal Finance
3 Useful Information Gathering
4 Domestic Affairs
5 Pleasure & Romance
6 Effective Work & Health

7 One to One Relationships
8 Questioning, Thinking & Deciding
9 External Influences / Education
10 Career Aspirations
11 Teamwork Activities
12 Unconscious Impulses

DECEMBER HIGHS AND LOWS

Here, I show how the rhythm of the Moon will affect you this month. Like the tide, your energies and abilities will rise and fall with its pattern. When it is above the date line, go-for-it. When it is below the line you should be resting.

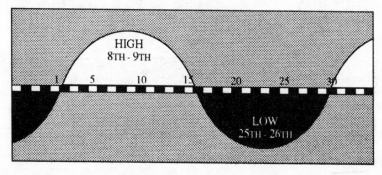

6 MONDAY
Moon Age 3 • Moon Sign Virgo

am ....

pm ....

Confounding your fiercest critics, you manage to make things work
out exactly as you have predicted. This might be fun, though if you
say "I told you so," it's also a very good way to go about making
enemies for later on. Far better to remain humble and pretend that
fate played a decisive hand in the way that things turned out.

7 TUESDAY
Moon Age Day 24 • Moon Sign Virgo

am ....

pm ....

A sound mixture of work and play appears to be the order of the day.
Several planets are pulling in your direction now, with Mercury
especially helping your powers of communication and others bolster-
ing your self-confidence. Look at your past ideas carefully before you
embark upon a process of overturning them.

8 WEDNESDAY
Moon Age Day 25 • Moon Sign Libra

am ....

pm ....

Mid-week madness takes you over as the more zany qualities of your
nature begin to bubble to the surface. Responsibility is something
that you are now quite happy to shy away from for a couple of days
and you may even be letting people make decisions at home that
have always been your own sphere of influence previously.

9 THURSDAY
Moon Age Day 26 • Moon Sign Libra

am ....

pm ....

Generally you are the sort of person who is not too difficult to live
with, so if people find you behaving unreasonably it's something that
they are apt to point out quite quickly. Such could be the case for a
while and falling out about the situation won't help at all. If you
have to, explain that you are as subject to human failings as anyone.

10 FRIDAY

Moon Age Day 27 • Moon Sign Scorpio

am ....

pm ....

There is no reason to feel out in the cold, merely because the presence of the lunar low demands a quieter and more contemplative Taurean for a couple of days. Priority decisions will still be right up your street, though it might be an idea to seek out extra advice before you take any situation too far.

11 SATURDAY

Moon Age Day 28 • Moon Sign Scorpio

am ....

pm ....

With the lunar low hovering in the background, this is not the best time to be embarking upon an adventure, though there is little or nothing to prevent you from planning one. Denials of the way your emotional nature is running won't be of much help and you would be well advised to speak the truth as you see it.

12 SUNDAY

Moon Age Day 29 • Moon Sign Sagittarius

am ....

pm ....

You were never one to worry too much about keeping up with the Jones' though there are certain trends about now that would seem to indicate that you are looking more carefully at your possessions. Time is knocking on so finanlise some social plans for Christmas and begin to compile all the endless lists, if you haven't started yet.

← NEGATIVE TREND							POSITIVE TREND →			
-5	-4	-3	-2	-1		+1	+2	+3	+4	+5
					LOVE					
					MONEY					
					LUCK					
					VITALITY					

13 MONDAY
Moon Age Day 0 • Moon Sign Sagittarius

am ....

pm ....

There is nothing at all to prevent you from choosing your life for yourself, even if some people presently think that they know better than you do how you should live it. Communication skills are increased and your joy for life outside of mundane considerations appears to know no bounds. Critics can be confounded this week.

14 TUESDAY
Moon Age Day 1 • Moon Sign Sagittarius

am ....

pm ....

It's consultation time because, thanks particularly to Venus, much of the remainder of the month shows how much you are taking the opinions of other people into account. Minor setbacks can be ignored or dealt with as and when they arise. Trying to look too far ahead is not a course of action to be encouraged just at the moment.

15 WEDNESDAY
Moon Age Day 2 • Moon Sign Capricorn

am ....

pm ....

The lure of the festive season is upon you now for certain. As usual you will want to create an ordered and happy sort of Christmas, including all the warmth that your sensitive soul can muster. Now is the time to be asking other people what they want and for building their ideas into your own scenario.

16 THURSDAY
Moon Age Day 3 • Moon Sign Capricorn

am ....

pm ....

There ought to be no shortage of help around now as efforts that you have made on behalf of others in the past are coming back to you with dividends. Your recent restlessness might well pay another short visit, which is why it is particularly important to be flexible and to make the most of small changes when they occur.

17 FRIDAY
Moon Age Day 4 • Moon Sign Aquarius

am ....

pm ....

Important communications come your way, and from a host of different directions. Mercury now not only allows you to be able to talk well but could also be making demands involving the written word. Perhaps it is time you were in touch with friends or relatives who are living away from the home; they may have news for you!

18 SATURDAY
Moon Age Day 5 • Moon Sign Aquarius

am ....

pm ....

Your own personal plans have the opportunity to mature properly, even if it does appear than an over eager world is trying to pressure you into doing things that go against the grain. Of course, some of your more adventurous and far reaching schemes will have to take a holiday, but only until the new year.

19 SUNDAY
Moon Age Day 6 • Moon Sign Pisces

am ....

pm ....

If you get the chance to clear the air between yourself and someone that you haven't been able to see eye to eye with in the recent past, there is no better time of year for burying the hatchet that this. Opt for a quiet Sunday if you have the chance and don't get wrapped up in other people's complicated plans.

← *NEGATIVE TREND*							*POSITIVE TREND* →			
-5	-4	-3	-2	-1		+1	+2	+3	+4	+5
					LOVE					
					MONEY					
					LUCK					
					VITALITY					

20 MONDAY
Moon Age Day 7 • Moon Sign Pisces

am ....

pm ....

This time and the planetary aspects that cover it really respond to a quiet role in you life. You would be much happier now just being allowed to get on with what pleases you and not finding yourself pestered to sort out problems that are not within your province at all. Check all documents carefully before committing yourself.

21 TUESDAY
Moon Age Day 8 • Moon Sign Pisces

am ....

pm ....

Romance falls under the spotlight for many Taureans now, mainly because you are in such a warm and sensitive mood yourself. People are likely to respond to this fact, and to the natural qualities inherent in the season. For most of you the social scene is beginning to speed up and, now is the time to achieve balance.

22 WEDNESDAY
Moon Age Day 9 • Moon Sign Aries

am ....

pm ....

It should be coming as second nature now to make other people as happy as you can, not that everyone is exactly anxious to fall in line with what you want to do. The behaviour of the odd individual is beyond your control and you should find that it is the way life looks as a whole that really influences you now.

23 THURSDAY
Moon Age Day 10 • Moon Sign Aries

am ....

pm ....

With final details sorted out as much as proves to be possible, it should now be a smooth, if busy, run up to Christmas Day. Your main concern is still likely to be the way that other people are enjoying themselves because that is where you derive your own enjoyment. You really are an unselfish Tauerean at the moment.

24 FRIDAY
Moon Age Day 11 • Moon Sign Taurus

am ....

pm ....

It could appear that anything other than the task in had is arriving to distract you now, and yet there is every planetary reason to believe that you should be generally happy, not least the arrival of the lunar high just in time for Christmas Eve. If ever you needed its energy giving light, you do at this time.

25 SATURDAY
Moon Age Day 12 • Moon Sign Taurus

am ....

pm ....

Serious matters are put behind you and with all the power of the Moon in your sign helping you all the way, you look towards a happy time, most of which is born out of watching other people enjoy themselves. There should be opportunities to give vent to some of your deepest emotions before this magical day is over.

26 SUNDAY
Moon Age Day 13 • Moon Sign Taurus

am ....

pm ....

Things will quieten down a little, though the lunar high is still offering its valued support and there are also indications that would favour travel for some children of Venus now. The only negative change is with regard to your temper, which could be shorter now if you are forced to deal with people who insist on being stupid. The simple advice is Don't!

← *NEGATIVE TREND*   *POSITIVE TREND* →

-5	-4	-3	-2	-1		+1	+2	+3	+4	+5
					LOVE					
					MONEY					
					LUCK					
					VITALITY					

27 MONDAY
Moon Age Day 14 • Moon Sign Gemini

am ....

pm ....

Now that much of the fuss has died down, you really should be thinking about getting some rest. People can fend for themselves more than you think, and after the last couple of days nobody could accuse you of having failed to work hard. In any case, it's only fair to let others spoil you for a while.

28 TUESDAY
Moon Age Day 15 • Moon Sign Gemini

am ....

pm ....

Taureans who are at work should find themselves facing a whole series of possibilities that could look very favourable in the fullness of time. All the same, at work or at home, it isn't wise under prevailing circumstances to make wholesale changes on the strength of rumours, or on account of what other people are saying.

29 WEDNESDAY
Moon Age Day 16 • Moon Sign Cancer

am ....

pm ....

Again Venus accents romance and things begin to hot up once more socially, that is if they have really cooled down at all. Confidence might be in short supply materially but certainly not from a personal point of view. In many respects, you now know what you want better than has been the case for several weeks.

30 THURSDAY
Moon Age Day 17 • Moon Sign Cancer

am ....

pm ....

As the last days of the year cause you to be somewhat reflective, you should find yourself able to look back on a period that has been both useful and interesting. What you haven't managed to achieve yet can easily be put on hold, so don't allow disappointments or nostalgia to get in the way of forward movement that has never stopped.

31 FRIDAY
Moon Age Day 18 • Moon Sign Leo

am ....

pm ....

Wave goodbye to 1993 and make you major resolution a desire to show the same care and compassion for other people that you have done this year. There are some exciting possibilities in store, not to mention a sensible continuation of your present efforts. With the right sort of belief in yourself, you can't go wrong!

1 SATURDAY
Moon Age Day 19 • Moon Sign Leo

am ....

pm ....

You may have to make major decisions and take some serious action regarding a family matter as the year opens. Certain pressures seem to weigh heavily upon you though what is accomplished today saves you much effort further down the line. There may not be the incentives to follow through New Year's resolutions now.

2 SUNDAY
Moon Age Day 20 • Moon Sign Virgo

am ....

pm ....

Your love life and leisure involvements bring out the best in you and you can be fulfilled in a number of different ways. Recreational pursuits prove to be very important and you genuinely show the ability to be yourself as confidence and enthusiasm appears in abundance. Avoid a conflict of interest with friends.

← *NEGATIVE TREND*   *POSITIVE TREND* →

-5	-4	-3	-2	-1		+1	+2	+3	+4	+5
					LOVE					
					MONEY					
					LUCK					
					VITALITY					

67

1994

YOUR MONTH AT A GLANCE

The twelve numbered boxes represent the important areas in your life. The key to the numbers you will find beneath the panel. A Sun above the number indicates that opportunities are around. A Cloud below the number, that you should be a bit defensive. Nothing above or below and life will be pretty ordinary.

1	2	3	4	5	6	7	8	9	10	11	12

KEY

1 Strength of Personality
2 Personal Finance
3 Useful Information Gathering
4 Domestic Affairs
5 Pleasure & Romance
6 Effective Work & Health

7 One to One Relationships
8 Questioning, Thinking & Deciding
9 External Influences / Education
10 Career Aspirations
11 Teamwork Activities
12 Unconscious Impulses

JANUARY HIGHS AND LOWS

Here, I show how the rhythm of the Moon will affect you this month. Like the tide, your energies and abilities will rise and fall with its pattern. When it is above the date line, go-for-it. When it is below the line you should be resting.

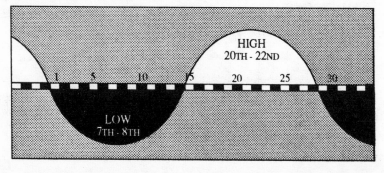

3 MONDAY   *Moon Age Day 21 • Moon Sign Virgo*

am ....

pm ....

At the start of the first real working week of the year, one to one relationships are enlivened by interesting debates and discussions. Taureans who are working today find new incentives coming along and a period when even the most unapproachable types are more considerate and less difficult to deal with.

4 TUESDAY   *Moon Age Day 22 • Moon Sign Libra*

am ....

pm ....

Expect some particularly happy news from a partner or from foreign parts. Social discussions are especially agreeable and rewarding whilst your outlook on life can be influenced especially in a financial sense by your partner or someone who clearly has your best interests at heart. Deep concentration can be difficult later in the day,

5 WEDNESDAY   *Moon Age Day 23 • Moon Sign Libra*

am ....

pm ....

The wheels of progress turn slowly on and in the main in a favourable way. Associates can be in a difficult or unapproachable mood, but this should not prevent progress as far as you are concerned personally. It will be difficult to check the behaviour of others and the best course of action is simply to let them be.

6 THURSDAY   *Moon Age Day 24 • Moon Sign Libra*

am ....

pm ....

Not a good time for taking risks in a business or a personal sense. The Moon is now in your opposite sign and you should do your best to prevent minor problems invading your daily life. Finish off mundane or routine tasks before you start with new ones, even if these feel rather unrewarding from a personal point of view.

7 FRIDAY

Moon Age Day 25 • Moon Sign Scorpio

am ....

pm ....

The lunar low stimulates emotional vulnerabilities and especially so
in one to one relationships. Try not to allow life to become a burden
for others because of your own demands and expectations. Even
apparent hold-ups or set-backs can turn out to be positive in the fullness of time and can not really be attributed to anyone's fault.

8 SATURDAY

Moon Age Day 26 • Moon Sign Scorpio

am ....

pm ....

Personal and professional involvements may be less satisfying than
you had desired, and you do need to feel very involved emotionally
with whatever is going on around you. There is more positivity in
your attitude and you should be able to find absorbing and interesting things to do. Tedious jobs should be performed early in the day.

9 SUNDAY

Moon Age Day 27 • Moon Sign Sagittarius

am ....

pm ....

Fall outs are possible in a social sense, due to a tendency to take
remarks personally. However, later in the day the shoe may be on
the other foot since it is you that is giving offence. Whilst feelings of
others need to be taken into consideration your own attitude
towards life is rather strange at present.

← *NEGATIVE TREND*   *POSITIVE TREND* →

-5	-4	-3	-2	-1				+1	+2	+3	+4	+5
						LOVE						
						MONEY						
						LUCK						
						VITALITY						

10 MONDAY
Moon Age Day 28 • Moon Sign Sagittarius

am ....

pm ....

It would be too easy, with the rather difficult association of the Sun and Neptune, to fall into the trap of believing everything you hear. Those around you may not be intentionally deceiving, but are still unlikely to offer you 100% of the truth. A rising tide of personal freedom sees you striking out in new directions.

11 TUESDAY
Moon Age Day 29 • Moon Sign Capricorn

am ....

pm ....

You find yourself unexpectedly on the go and any long journeys that you have to make should prove to be especially rewarding. New contacts can be made with unusual or unconventional types of people who have a powerful effect on you. Life can be full of contradictions on a personal level.

12 WEDNESDAY
Moon Age Day 0 • Moon Sign Capricorn

am ....

pm ....

Certainly a good day for getting down to basics and for settling any misunderstandings that exist in your vicinity. Because you are communicating clearly and logically, those closest to you are willing to listen to what you have to say. You really do exhibit a human touch and this also reflects on the romantic aspects of your life.

13 THURSDAY
Moon Age Day 1 • Moon Sign Aquarius

am ....

pm ....

Your own social interests could upset your partner today and so you need to make an effort to understand what might be on their mind. Travel plans can go slightly awry and so you need to work out details very carefully. A time to expect the unexpected and to ride the changes of life which nearly all turn out in your favour in the end.

14 FRIDAY

Moon Age Day 2 • Moon Sign Aquarius

am ....

pm ....

Those in authority place you in a rather taxing role today, but this does at least offer you the opportunity to show how efficient you are. Efforts today can lead towards a better destination that you had expected and so you will be doing all you can to prove your worth in every respect. Home situations are relaxing.

15 SATURDAY

Moon Age Day 3 • Moon Sign Pisces

am ....

pm ....

Group efforts and co-operation of all sorts pay dividends. Help comes in from the outside world and provides excellent progress generally. Social involvements provide a happy atmosphere where you can forget about the cares of the world and concentrate more on your own personal desires. Do not keep too busy today.

16 SUNDAY

Moon Age Day 4 • Moon Sign Pisces

am ....

pm ....

A favourable association between the Sun and Venus, the planet of love, sees you reaching an emotional and mental peak. With every opportunity to feel good and optimistic about the future, high expectations that you have of life tend to be realistic and sensible. Personally, it 's important not to allow your imagination to run away.

← *NEGATIVE TREND*   *POSITIVE TREND* →

-5	-4	-3	-2	-1			+1	+2	+3	+4	+5
					LOVE						
					MONEY						
					LUCK						
					VITALITY						

17 MONDAY
Moon Age Day 5 • Moon Sign Pisces

am ....

pm ....

Information regarding professional involvements starts the week favourably and future plans put you in the picture allowing you to lay down new ground rules for your own life. Beware, loved ones could be feeling neglected and in need of special attention that you are able to give. Former associates begin to become close friends.

18 TUESDAY
Moon Age Day 6 • Moon Sign Aries

am ....

pm ....

It could be that you prefer a lower profile today than has been the case recently, concentrating on private matters and mulling over situations from the past. However, despite your need for privacy and independence, you should be careful not to shut others out totally. This is particularly true in the case of your partner.

19 WEDNESDAY
Moon Age Day 7 • Moon Sign Aries

am ....

pm ....

You could find yourself to be popular in the most unlikely situations today, but be careful not to be misled by new contacts who, though stimulating, may prove to be rather distracting too. Not all the compliments you receive from other people prove to be equally valid and it is important to sort out the wheat from the chaff.

20 THURSDAY
Moon Age Day 8 • Moon Sign Taurus

am ....

pm ....

The arrival of the lunar high represents the beginning of a new mini-cycle when fresh starts become ever more likely. This is especially true with regard to your personal life and since luck is also on your side, you can even afford to take the odd chance. However, many of the benefits of the period may not prove to be particularly obvious.

21 FRIDAY
Moon Age Day 9 • Moon Sign Taurus

am ....

pm ....

Energy and enthusiasm now reaches an all time high. Not only can you be inspired by almost anything that is going on around you, but you have a profound effect on the opinions and attitudes of others. Taking risks could prove to be fortunate, though keep these to a minimum, for the moment.

22 SATURDAY
Moon Age Day 10 • Moon Sign Taurus

am ....

pm ....

Opportunities that arise today should be turned to your advantage. Most of the people surrounding you seem only too willing to do you as many favours as they can, though be careful to ensure that their motives are sound. A good time to think long-term and to make the most of friendship.

23 SUNDAY
Moon Age Day 11 • Moon Sign Gemini

am ....

pm ....

You seem to be enjoying a particularly high profile in the outside world. The only danger here is that you are inclined to take on too much in the way of commitments. Confrontations, particularly with powerful types should be avoided and conciliation is always the best course of action for you at present. Contrary opinions are possible.

← *NEGATIVE TREND*   *POSITIVE TREND* →

-5	-4	-3	-2	-1			+1	+2	+3	+4	+5
					LOVE						
					MONEY						
					LUCK						
					VITALITY						

24 MONDAY   *Moon Age Day 12 • Moon Sign Gemini*

am ....

pm ....

There is little doubt that you are relying heavily on others, but opinions and views may not conform to your own. However, there is much good advice about and personal help is on offer. A more self-reliant approach is required and this tends to show later in the day. Too much advice acted upon at present can prove to be troublesome.

25 TUESDAY   *Moon Age Day 13 • Moon Sign Cancer*

am ....

pm ....

All travel, appointments, meetings or routine endeavours can suffer from minor misunderstandings. Be sure to put your point of view across clearly and in a concise manner. News received from friends or associates can prove to be something of a let down, but you shouldn't allow this to affect your work.

26 WEDNESDAY   *Moon Age Day 14 • Moon Sign Cancer*

am ....

pm ....

With an important association between the planets Mercury and Neptune, there is a degree of uncertainty regarding business or professional aspects of your life. Take note - it would be unwise to make any important moves unless you are absolutely certain of your direction in life. Keeping to a tried and tested path is important.

27 THURSDAY   *Moon Age Day 15 • Moon Sign Cancer*

am ....

pm ....

Conflicting interests attend your life now with career and family responsibilities at odds with each other. From the very start of the day it is important to get your priorities right and attend to the issues that mean the most to you at any particular point in time. A close family member may require some emotional support.

28 FRIDAY

Moon Age Day 16 • Moon Sign Leo

am ....

pm ....

Mars enters your solar tenth house bringing new enthusiasms and a more positive approach to career prospects. Major short term plans start to come to fruition, though you won't take kindly to an authoritarian attitude on the part of others and work best as your own boss at present. Beware of allowing minor difficulties to grow.

29 SATURDAY

Moon Age Day 17 • Moon Sign Leo

am ....

pm ....

Social atmosphere is particularly good and excitement seems to lie around every corner. The most important tasks that you come across seem to be a labour of love and major objectives may now come within your reach. Those Taureans who are thinking about a move of house should look around quite carefully at the present.

30 SUNDAY

Moon Age Day 18 • Moon Sign Virgo

am ....

pm ....

Don't be in too much of a hurry to achieve all of your objectives at the same time. Mistakes are easily made and so it is important to use your logical, steady and serene approach to life wherever possible. Taurean patience is famous and although it may be lacking a little at present, the basis of your nature remains the same.

← NEGATIVE TREND   POSITIVE TREND →

-5	-4	-3	-2	-1		+1	+2	+3	+4	+5
					LOVE					
					MONEY					
					LUCK					
					VITALITY					

31 MONDAY
Moon Age Day 1 9 • Moon Sign Virgo

am ....

pm ....

Although you are very busy in a practical sense, it's social interests that receive an additional boost with little Mercury entering your solar eleventh house. As a result you could find yourself to be much in demand from friends and even more casual associates. Although you are in good company don't allow this to sidetrack you.

1 TUESDAY
Moon Age Day 20 • Moon Sign Libra

am ....

pm ....

Give and take are both important today, though not half so essential as doing the things that are personally important to you. You won't get very far trying to please everyone and when all is said and done you are expected to take the initiative in any case.

2 WEDNESDAY
Moon Age Day 21 • Moon Sign Libra

am ....

pm ....

The lunar low is certain to slow things down a little and so trying to accomplish major objectives could prove to be rather difficult today. Take life one step at a time and leave all important decisions either to your partner, or until a later date if at all possible. Most important of all, ensure that you get plenty of rest.

3 THURSDAY
Moon Age Day 22 • Moon Sign Scorpio

am ....

pm ....

Minor set-backs occur which appear to have no immediate solution and the best course of action would be to avoid thinking about them at all. Continue to have faith in the eventual positive outcome of personal objectives and you can't go far wrong. Concentrate on those things which are within your grasp now.

4 FRIDAY
Moon Age Day 23 • Moon Sign Scorpio

am ....

pm ....

Getting through to your partner or loved one is not without some effort. However, the Moon is in your solar eighth house and times are looking better, so even if it appears that others are being difficult, you should be able to bring them round to your point of view eventually. Socialising with newcomers in your life is important.

5 SATURDAY
Moon Age Day 24 • Moon Sign Sagittarius

am ....

pm ....

It seems as if your personal judgement is called into question by people in your immediate vicinity. The last thing you should do is take a 'know-it-all' approach. Your imagination is stimulated and you grow stronger in your ability to visualise a brighter and better future for yourself and for those around you.

6 SUNDAY
Moon Age Day 25 • Moon Sign Sagittarius

am ....

pm ....

General energy and the level of your ego are both high. Skill shows itself in anything that you undertake, though if you are out to seek praise or compliments you could end up being rather disappointed. Outwitting those who appear to work against your best interests seems to be rather easier than normal at present.

← *NEGATIVE TREND*   *POSITIVE TREND* →

-5	-4	-3	-2	-1		+1	+2	+3	+4	+5
					LOVE					
					MONEY					
					LUCK					
					VITALITY					

1994

YOUR MONTH AT A GLANCE

The twelve numbered boxes represent the important areas in your life. The key to the numbers you will find beneath the panel. A Sun above the number indicates that opportunities are around. A Cloud below the number, that you should be a bit defensive. Nothing above or below and life will be pretty ordinary.

1	2	3	4	5	6	7	8	9	10	11	12

FEBRUARY HIGHS AND LOWS

Here, I show how the rhythm of the Moon will affect you this month. Like the tide, your energies and abilities will rise and fall with its pattern. When it is above the date line, go-for-it. When it is below the line you should be resting.

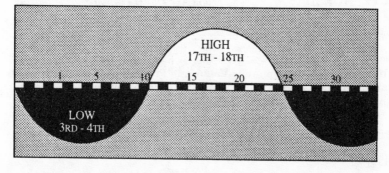

7 MONDAY   *Moon Age Day 26 • Moon Sign Capricorn*

am ....

pm ....

All things being equal, you need to be free to explore the world at large today, despite the fact that professional involvements may not permit you to do so. At the very least, you should try to find some interesting leisure outlets, and to fulfil the requirement for mental stimulation that is too much a part of you at present.

8 TUESDAY   *Moon Age Day 27 • Moon Sign Capricorn*

am ....

pm ....

Opportunities come along to get away from it all as social invitations beckon. All encounters with groups or associations of other people can be turned to your advantage and would certainly help to make life a little lighter or carefree. A positive attitude towards work can bring great benefits.

9 WEDNESDAY   *Moon Age Day 28 • Moon Sign Aquarius*

am ....

pm ....

You certainly could not be accused of taking other people for granted today, though perhaps you are not showing as much attention as you could to your own needs and wants. On a personal level, confrontations are likely, especially if you consider that others are bringing your nature into disrepute.

10 THURSDAY   *Moon Age Day 0 • Moon Sign Aquarius*

am ....

pm ....

An association of the planets Venus and Pluto shows how much your mind could be working in the past. There is a negative quality to this tendency at present, whilst on the other side of the coin, talking about your feelings to your partner or to a close friend could be seen as being distinctly healthy. This may still be true, even if the subject matter isn't too pleasant.

11 FRIDAY

Moon Age Day 1 • Moon Sign Aquarius

am ....

pm ....

The best way to square situations with people who may not have been on your wavelength recently, is to meet them on a social footing. Although earlier in the week you showed great care, speaking your mind at present need not create particular problems. In fact, others will be expecting it of you.

12 SATURDAY

Moon Age Day 2 • Moon Sign Pisces

am ....

pm ....

With the Sun strong in your solar tenth house, there are favourable events for the weekend associated with either personal or professional schemes. Your leadership qualities are in great demand and it would appear that those around you are relying on your help and judgement. Make the most of the fact.

13 SUNDAY

Moon Age Day 3 • Moon Sign Pisces

am ....

pm ....

Venus, your ruling planet, now enters your solar eleventh house bringing a noticeable boost to your popularity. You show a marked desire to be friendly to almost everyone you come across and acquaintances start to turn into friends as the days pass. You may also notice that you become more concerned with justice.

← *NEGATIVE TREND*   *POSITIVE TREND* →

-5	-4	-3	-2	-1			+1	+2	+3	+4	+5
					LOVE						
					MONEY						
					LUCK						
					VITALITY						

14 MONDAY   *Moon Age Day 4 • Moon Sign Aries*

am ....

pm ....

The susceptibility you show to the influence of others may not be entirely healthy and this will be particularly true in the case of those who have grandiose schemes. Don't commit yourself to anything until you have weighed up the pros and cons of the situation clearly.

15 TUESDAY   *Moon Age Day 5 • Moon Sign Aries*

am ....

pm ....

An aspect between the planets Mars and Jupiter in your chart now has an enlivening effect on one to one relationships. Your partner may be more boisterous than usual, so if you are expecting a period of peace today, you can probably forget it. However, there is excellent progress to be made in a career sense.

16 WEDNESDAY   *Moon Age Day 6 • Moon Sign Aries*

am ....

pm ....

Along comes the lunar high, bringing positive aspects with regard to personal projects and practical plans that you may have in hand at present. A little luck comes your way and most events go more or less as planned. Remember, however, that this is a time for doing, not merely sitting back and enjoying what life has to offer.

17 THURSDAY   *Moon Age Day 7 • Moon Sign Taurus*

am ....

pm ....

Probably the best time of the month to put new ideas into operation, be they small or large. Your powers of persuasion are on the increase and can bring round even influential figures who show themselves as being even more responsive to your ideas now, than would have been the case in the past. Your love life could prove to be exciting.

18 FRIDAY
Moon Age Day 8 • Moon Sign Taurus

am ....

pm ....

The lunar high is still around, bringing you now to a physical peak, during which you can accomplish objectives efficiently and optimistically. Private matters can bring great satisfaction and this would also be a favourable time for some limited speculation of a financial nature.

19 SATURDAY
Moon Age Day 9 • Moon Sign Gemini

am ....

pm ....

Today the Sun enters your solar eleventh house, taking over from where the lunar high has left off in terms of pushing your life forward. This should be the commencement of a new period of reward for all group or team work involvements. Much of the effort will be down to you, so get cracking.

20 SUNDAY
Moon Age Day 10 • Moon Sign Gemini

am ....

pm ....

Some improvement is possible where finances have been difficult previously. You will however have to work fairly hard in pursuit of potential achievements. The problem seems to be that there is no one else to rely on but yourself at the present time. Chatty and conversational, you should enjoy a high profile social Sunday.

← NEGATIVE TREND							POSITIVE TREND →			
-5	-4	-3	-2	-1			+1	+2	+3	+4	+5
				LOVE						
				MONEY						
				LUCK						
				VITALITY						

21 MONDAY
Moon Age Day 11 • Moon Sign Gemini

am ....

pm ....

There is a possibility that today you will have to deal with people you are not particularly fond of. All the same try to maintain an objective view of life and keep personal feelings to a minimum where possible. The best of all attitude for you is to live and let live at present, though circumstances could make this difficult to follow.

22 TUESDAY
Moon Age Day 12 • Moon Sign Cancer

am ....

pm ....

All associations with travel, meetings or appointments of any kind keep you busy and on the go right now. Rewards of one kind or another are in the offing and though there may be minor setbacks professionally, you should avoid allowing this to make you rush your fences. A good time to go where life leads.

23 WEDNESDAY
Moon Age Day 13 • Moon Sign Cancer

am ....

pm ....

The general domestic atmosphere today can be affected by the complaints or disagreements coming from the direction of people you know well. It could seem that there is no avoiding conflict and this being the case, it would be better to get arguments out of the way as quickly as possible. Definitely a testing time.

24 THURSDAY
Moon Age Day 14 • Moon Sign Leo

am ....

pm ....

A planetary association between Venus and Jupiter affects relationships and your social life in a harmonious way. There is a significant amount of compromise about between yourself and those people who are important in your life. There could even be new relationships or friendships in the making and some Taureans should expect the beginning of a new and important social phase.

25 FRIDAY
Moon Age Day 15 • Moon Sign Leo

am ....

pm ....

What you have to say to others in a professional situation could easily be misunderstood. It would be useful to explain yourself fully, lest those around you become suspicious of your behaviour. Even more than would be the case normally, you should be honest and forthright, both in your thinking and in what you do.

26 SATURDAY
Moon Age Day 16 • Moon Sign Virgo

am ....

pm ....

The Moon in your solar fifth house, stirs up the romantic side of your nature, which in the case of a Taurean is never far below the surface in any case. This would be an excellent day for telling someone special just how you feel about them. Close encounters of all kinds are more favourable now.

27 SUNDAY
Moon Age Day 17 • Moon Sign Virgo

am ....

pm ....

Be careful of any hasty decision making at work, simply because it seems that you have all the facts. In reality you probably don't. An offer of help from a friend may be rejected, though you should ask yourself whether you are being wise in turning away the chance to offer assistance.

← *NEGATIVE TREND*   *POSITIVE TREND* →

-5	-4	-3	-2	-1			+1	+2	+3	+4	+5
			▓		LOVE						
				▓	MONEY						
					LUCK	▓					
					VITALITY	▓					

28 MONDAY
Moon Age Day 18 • Moon Sign Libra

am ....

pm ....

Despite minor ups and downs, the progress that you make in a career sense tends to be favourable. If life is demanding, then you tend to enjoy it all the more, so long as you are left to get on with things in your own way. Where social discussions are concerned, it would be wise to avoid arguments.

1 TUESDAY
Moon Age Day 19 • Moon Sign Libra

am ....

pm ....

Not a good time to be over reacting to minor mishaps in your everyday life, despite the fact that the Moon occupies its low position for the month. It is true that your energy is in short supply, but either your partner or a friend should be willing to handle major issues for today if possible.

2 WEDNESDAY
Moon Age Day 20 • Moon Sign Scorpio

am ....

pm ....

Getting others to see things your way is not easy, but the effort required to do so can definitely be worthwhile. In fact it could be suggested that your influence over others is much higher than you would possibly expect. Try to keep life on a simple basis, not expecting too much either of yourself or those around you.

3 THURSDAY
Moon Age Day 21 • Moon Sign Scorpio

am ....

pm ....

With one or two unexpected set-backs early in the day, once again you need to keep an open mind and probably to rely on your intuition which is still strong. Patience is certainly the virtue you are looking for at present, and you need to keep faith in any end result. Most annoying of all today, it could appear that everyone else is getting their own way except you.

4 FRIDAY
Moon Age Day 22 • Moon Sign Sagittarius

am ....

pm ....

A definite return of high spirits today, and you should feel capable of handling almost anything, especially in professional matters. Intimate relationships are rewarding, but you need to bear in mind the feelings of a sensitive individual, possibly a partner who could have been listening too closely to a throw-away statement.

5 SATURDAY
Moon Age Day 23 • Moon Sign Sagittarius

am ....

pm ....

Team-work issues and group objectives bring a little good fortune into your life as it becomes easier to obtain your objectives. Newcomers on the social scene have a great deal to offer you, both in terms of goodwill and co-operation. Confidence to do what you want for the weekend is certainly not lacking and incentives are good.

6 SUNDAY
Moon Age Day 24 • Moon Sign Capricorn

am ....

pm ....

Positive highlights occur with regard to social discussions. You can get along with others in an easy going way, but don't neglect the important details of practical matters. A too relaxed approach might bring problems later on, so pay attention to what is going on around you.

← NEGATIVE TREND								POSITIVE TREND →			
-5	-4	-3	-2	-1			+1	+2	+3	+4	+5
					LOVE						
					MONEY						
					LUCK						
					VITALITY						

1994

YOUR MONTH AT A GLANCE

The twelve numbered boxes represent the important areas in your life. The key to the numbers you will find beneath the panel. A Sun above the number indicates that opportunities are around. A Cloud below the number, that you should be a bit defensive. Nothing above or below and life will be pretty ordinary.

1	2	3	4	5	6	7	8	9	10	11	12

KEY

1 Strength of Personality
2 Personal Finance
3 Useful Information Gathering
4 Domestic Affairs
5 Pleasure & Romance
6 Effective Work & Health

7 One to One Relationships
8 Questioning, Thinking & Deciding
9 External Influences / Education
10 Career Aspirations
11 Teamwork Activities
12 Unconscious Impulses

MARCH HIGHS AND LOWS

Here, I show how the rhythm of the Moon will affect you this month. Like the tide, your energies and abilities will rise and fall with its pattern. When it is above the date line, go-for-it. When it is below the line you should be resting.

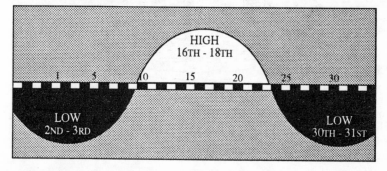

HIGH
16TH - 18TH

LOW
2ND - 3RD

LOW
30TH - 31ST

7 MONDAY
Moon Age Day 25 • Moon Sign Capricorn

am ....

pm ....

Mars is strong in your chart now, and so you will be taking the lead in initiating new social contacts or perhaps assuming a leading role where groups of people are concerned. You do show a greater than usual tendency to stir up conflict when none really need exist, so beware of your own argumentative potential.

8 TUESDAY
Moon Age Day 26 • Moon Sign Capricorn

am ....

pm ....

Though career and personal plans mostly go your way at this time, you may have some rather unrealistic ambitions or expectations. With a slight tendency to blind faith, or false optimism, all the dreaming in the world will probably get you nowhere at present.

9 WEDNESDAY
Moon Age Day 27 • Moon Sign Aquarius

am ....

pm ....

There is a slight lull in one to one relationships as Venus enters your solar twelfth house. In personal attachments, it could be difficult to get your own way, which is why a more casual sort of mixing seems to be preferred at present. You can see the faults in others all too easily. Time spent alone is, generally speaking, spent well.

10 THURSDAY
Moon Age Day 28 • Moon Sign Aquarius

am ....

pm ....

Circumstances turn around as the contact between Venus and Mars increases the potential for social happenings, which stimulate and raise your spirits. All aspects of pleasure look good, even though loved ones could be a little difficult to handle. It might be suggested that some time spent away from those closest to you could do all concerned a certain amount of good.

90

11 FRIDAY
Moon Age Day 29 • Moon Sign Pisces

am ....

pm ....

Invitations coming from the direction of friends should be looked at carefully before being dismissed out of hand. Whatever you decide to embark upon at present, there should be a significant amount of enjoyment involved. This will be an excellent time to throw a party, or for coming to terms with a romantic proposal.

12 SATURDAY
Moon Age Day 0 • Moon Sign Pisces

am ....

pm ....

Planetary indications today, with Mercury contacting the Planet Uranus, show that speedy decisions are essential. Hesitation is certainly to be avoided and a final judgement can be made regarding specific plans or intentions. Moves made towards professional changes respond to some extra thought.

13 SUNDAY
Moon Age Day 1 • Moon Sign Aries

am ....

pm ....

There are friendly and generous gestures surrounding you on all sides. A good Sunday for reaping the goodwill that you had previously shown yourself, and also an excellent time for getting out and about, either short or long term journeys proving to be equally favourable.

← NEGATIVE TREND　　　　　　　　　　*POSITIVE TREND →*

-5	-4	-3	-2	-1		+1	+2	+3	+4	+5
					LOVE					
					MONEY					
					LUCK					
					VITALITY					

14 MONDAY
Moon Age Day 2 • Moon Sign Aries

am ....

pm ....

Partners can be quite demanding at the start of a new working week, though most of your attention needs to be turned towards career prospects and general practicalities. When faced with a number of uncertainties, you may be inclined to opt for the devil you know.

15 TUESDAY
Moon Age Day 3 • Moon Sign Aries

am ....

pm ....

Along comes the lunar high, the best time of the month to put anything new into action. You could notice a favourable interlude with regard to business enterprise etc. All social involvements also bring out the best in you, in fact it wouldn't be going too far to suggest that you are the star attraction.

16 WEDNESDAY
Moon Age Day 4 • Moon Sign Taurus

am ....

pm ....

If ever you had the feeling that you could handle almost anything, today is such a time. With a spirit of high confidence you push forward in most spheres and should be keeping an eye out for advantageous positions at work. Lady Luck is apt to be on your side and the path ahead shines out clearly.

17 THURSDAY
Moon Age Day 5 • Moon Sign Taurus

am ....

pm ....

The main advantage now, with the Moon still occupying a favourable position as far as you are concerned, lies in your ability to talk influential figures round to your point of view. Any small gamble should work out to your advantage, as luck is still on your side. Conventional thinking tends to be out of the window for the moment.

18 FRIDAY   *Moon Age Day 6 • Moon Sign Taurus*

am ....

pm ....

The Moon enters your solar second house and could bring with it unexpected financial demands. Whenever possible, settle these as soon as is reasonable, or there could be problems further down the line. Many Taureans will see this as a day where tests of strength come from a number of different directions.

19 SATURDAY   *Moon Age Day 7 • Moon Sign Gemini*

am ....

pm ....

Little Mercury enters your solar eleventh house, bringing a sure indication that social meetings and get-togethers are enlivened. You show a cheerful face to the world, can be particularly good in conversation and in all social mixing. Very definitely a good time for making general progress.

20 SUNDAY   *Moon Age Day 8 • Moon Sign Gemini*

am ....

pm ....

The routines of everyday life should now be plain sailing. True to the quieter side of Taurus, you can be content with the simpler things of life, though perhaps a more determined and ambitious approach would not go amiss in professional arrangements of any sort. This could be a day of sunshine and showers in personal attachments.

← *NEGATIVE TREND*   *POSITIVE TREND* →

-5	-4	-3	-2	-1		+1	+2	+3	+4	+5
			▓		LOVE		▓			
					MONEY		▓			
				▓	LUCK					
					VITALITY	▓				

21 MONDAY
Moon Age Day 9 • Moon Sign Cancer

am ....

pm ....

A slight lack of influence over others is an important consideration at the start of this working week. Don't be afraid to play a significant role in life and avoid being inclined to hold back your point of view, simply because it doesn't agree with that of those around you. Negative thoughts should be put away.

22 TUESDAY
Moon Age Day 10 • Moon Sign Cancer

am ....

pm ....

Not everything that you see when you look at your partner or close relatives turns out to be exactly true, so don't be surprised if you are accused of viewing your immediate world through rose coloured glasses. It is all to easy at the moment to put others on a pedestal and to suffer some disillusion further down the line as a result.

23 WEDNESDAY
Moon Age Day 11 • Moon Sign Leo

am ....

pm ....

Domestic matters and happenings on the family scene contribute to a feeling of security and peace of mind, because at present you need to be amongst familiar people, places and ideas. A too hesitant approach to business may need to be overcome and you really can put your mind to the task in hand.

24 THURSDAY
Moon Age Day 12 • Moon Sign Leo

am ....

pm ....

Be careful of who you challenge in social encounters. A reversal in trends indicates better professional prospects, but some uncertainty once the working day is over. You might be held in disfavour by people who normally have a positive view of you, and so it could be seen as being providential to stick to those individuals you know the best. Don't allow these points to prevent you speaking your mind.

25 FRIDAY

Moon Age Day 13 • Moon Sign Leo

am ....

pm ....

All romantic and pleasure activities are high on your agenda. The only thing you need be wary of is a little over-confidence regarding physical luxury etc. Loved ones can make life very pleasurable, though in some ways you may be inclined to attract the wrong sort of people towards you. Routines can be something of a drag.

26 SATURDAY

Moon Age Day 14 • Moon Sign Virgo

am ....

pm ....

The Sun is now strong in your solar twelfth house, so that the sympathy that you show for the emotional problems of others becomes quite remarkable. Much of the weekend may be given over to sorting things out on behalf of friends or family members, and there is just a slight danger that you will tire yourself.

27 SUNDAY

Moon Age Day 15 • Moon SignVirgo

am ....

pm ....

You really cannot afford to be too giving today. Give others an inch and they are apt to take a yard. Interpreting this as too much humility and self sacrifice could cost you dearly. By all means show concern for the world at large, but just for once it is important to put yourself first. A continued reliance on one particular person could prove to be fairly tiring and difficult.

← NEGATIVE TREND							POSITIVE TREND →			
-5	-4	-3	-2	-1			+1	+2	+3	+4	+5
					LOVE						
					MONEY						
					LUCK						
					VITALITY						

28 MONDAY
Moon Age Day 16 • Moon Sign Libra

am ....

pm ....

The wheels of general progress are turning positively as far as you are concerned, though you might be over-concerned at the moment with a particular problem. It will be no bad thing to stay in the dark regarding specific issues at the beginning of this working week, as the light of reason and common sense starts to flood in.

29 TUESDAY
Moon Age Day 17 • Moon Sign Libra

am ....

pm ....

With the lunar low comes a tendency for strong words from you and possibly going in the direction of your partner. However, choose what you have to say carefully, as this is hardly the most beneficial time to be speaking your mind. Keep life as simple as possible and take time out to recharge your batteries.

30 WEDNESDAY
Moon Age Day 18 • Moon Sign Scorpio

am ....

pm ....

Minor let-downs should be forgotten as soon as they occur, as you proceed towards tasks and responsibilities that you know you can fulfil. You may not get a great deal of emotional fulfilment from life at present, but you can still maintain a steady progress and a general interest in what is going on around you.

31 THURSDAY
Moon Age Day 19 • Moon Sign Scorpio

am ....

pm ....

Disagreements or disappointments regarding joint financial matters indicate that you should take a listening approach. Although you have to get by with little emotional or financial support from others you are very much influenced by a rising tide of confidence within your own nature. Creature comforts also take on significantly less importance as the day wears on.

1 FRIDAY
Moon Age Day 20 • Moon Sign Sagittarius

am ....

pm ....

A new acquaintance, or casual contact, could have an attractive proposition to put to you today. If the implications of this are short term, then it would be sensible to go ahead. However, if you are making plans for the longer term future, stop to think carefully, possibly taking the advice of a disinterested third party.

2 SATURDAY
Moon Age Day 21 • Moon Sign Sagittarius

am ....

pm ....

Venus enters your solar second house bringing a boost to one on one relationships in a way that you view them. Some Taureans can now expect the beginnings of a romance, or a deep friendship. You look for and find the agreeable sides of those around you and have a very sensitive touch when dealing with individuals. Be sure to use it.

3 SUNDAY
Moon Age Day 22 • Moon Sign Capricorn

am ....

pm ....

Talks or deeper discussions with personal friends, can lift today significantly. Information coming in is likely to be informative or educational in some way and there could be good news arriving regarding personal plans for travel or journeys of any sort. All in all, this should prove to be a useful sort of day.

← NEGATIVE TREND   POSITIVE TREND →

-5	-4	-3	-2	-1			+1	+2	+3	+4	+5
					LOVE						
					MONEY						
					LUCK						
					VITALITY						

1994

YOUR MONTH AT A GLANCE

The twelve numbered boxes represent the important areas in your life. The key to the numbers you will find beneath the panel. A Sun above the number indicates that opportunities are around. A Cloud below the number, that you should be a bit defensive. Nothing above or below and life will be pretty ordinary.

1	2	3	4	5	6	7	8	9	10	11	12

(Suns appear above boxes 2, 5, and 12; Clouds appear below boxes 7 and 8)

KEY

1 Strength of Personality
2 Personal Finance
3 Useful Information Gathering
4 Domestic Affairs
5 Pleasure & Romance
6 Effective Work & Health

7 One to One Relationships
8 Questioning, Thinking & Deciding
9 External Influences / Education
10 Career Aspirations
11 Teamwork Activities
12 Unconscious Impulses

APRIL HIGHS AND LOWS

Here, I show how the rhythm of the Moon will affect you this month. Like the tide, your energies and abilities will rise and fall with its pattern. When it is above the date line, go-for-it. When it is below the line you should be resting.

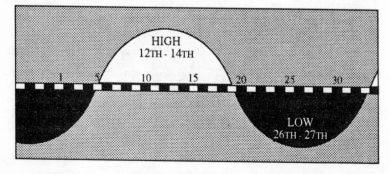

HIGH
12TH - 14TH

LOW
26TH - 27TH

4 MONDAY
Moon Age Day 23 · Moon Sign Capricorn

am ....

pm ....

The people you work with, and especially superiors, are more than likely to support, or show approval for some of your dearest plans. This fact alone can put you in a position of some influence, though might cause a slight amount of animosity from people who consider themselves to be more in-the-know than you are.

5 TUESDAY
Moon Age Day 24 · Moon Sign Aquarius

am ....

pm ....

With Mercury and the planet Neptune in close association now, social happenings provide light relief from more mundane and practical responsibilities. You can afford to be a little more assertive when it comes to social arrangements that you are responsible for and indeed do not leave things to chance.

6 WEDNESDAY
Moon Age Day 25 · Moon Sign Aquarius

am ....

pm ....

The Sun is strong in your solar twelfth house and for once you are more likely to retire into your own shell rather than have too much to do with the world at large. Imaginatively, you also want to be wrapped up in your own world. It would be advantageous this week to find some time to be absolutely alone, where you can unwind.

7 THURSDAY
Moon Age Day 26 · Moon Sign Pisces

am ....

pm ....

Stay away from divided loyalties whenever it proves possible to do so. Even relatives could challenge your sincerity and you won't be reluctant to speak your mind in return, or to tell others how you feel about life generally. If you have to let someone down do it carefully, though a new appraisal of life might mean that you are too busy to show the level of consideration to others than is often the case.

8 FRIDAY
Moon Age Day 27 • Moon Sign Pisces

am ....

pm ....

Your own self image is very important, perhaps too much so at present with Venus and Saturn making you too concerned with what looks right. Carried too far, this attitude can have a poor effect on your efficiency especially at work. In all aspects of life now, there is a tendency to be making mountains out of molehills.

9 SATURDAY
Moon Age Day 28 • Moon Sign Pisces

am ....

pm ....

The weekend brings a change in events and today is excellent for all imaginative or creative work. Be careful though, since tasks regarding concentration and logic can suffer. Although it is difficult to think positively, it is not hard to act with imagination. A fine balancing act - but one that you should manage with a little care.

10 SUNDAY
Moon Age Day 29 • Moon Sign Aries

am ....

pm ....

A friend provides much encouragement regarding personal interests and you can now do better regarding social groups and casual acquaintances of almost any sort. Deeper and more emotional ties take something of a back seat as your light touch on life proves to be in evidence. Not a day to be solemn.

← *NEGATIVE TREND*   *POSITIVE TREND* →

-5	-4	-3	-2	-1		+1	+2	+3	+4	+5
					LOVE					
					MONEY					
					LUCK					
					VITALITY					

11 MONDAY
Moon Age Day 0 • Moon Sign Aries

am ....

pm ....

The duties that are an integral part of your life, plus the obligations that you feel towards others, can be quite tiresome at the beginning of what turns out to be a busy and generally effective week. Try to push one or two of these responsibilities towards the back of your mind if it proves possible to do so.

12 TUESDAY
Moon Age Day 1 • Moon Sign Taurus

am ....

pm ....

With the lunar high arriving today, your energy and enthusiasm returns in abundance. In fact you could be accused of being quite boisterous today. Any action that you take is apt to show a positive influence on others as you get your partner or friends to join in the fun. Professional opportunities can come like a bolt from the blue.

13 WEDNESDAY
Moon Age Day 2 • Moon Sign Taurus

am ....

pm ....

Those Taureans who now find themselves with free time on their hands should spend an hour or two considering important plans for the future. Whenever the chance occurs to set the ball rolling in a new direction, you will want to be involved. If you have to take a minor risk of any kind, now might be the best time to do so.

14 THURSDAY
Moon Age Day 3 • Moon Sign Taurus

am ....

pm ....

Beware of minor mishaps brought about as a result of impatience, especially in or around the home. Mars is in your solar twelfth house and this also brings strong emotions, perhaps even a little resentment concerning personal matters. The very best way to proceed now is to be willing to get things off your chest, though it is by no means certain that those close to you would agree.

101

15 FRIDAY

Moon Age Day 4 • Moon Sign Gemini

am ....

pm ....

With a stronger emphasis on luxury than on the more creative potential within your nature, you will also want to find comfort within your home. These aspects can bring out both your best and worst qualities. However don't be tempted to shirk your responsibilities, simply because you feel so laid back personally.

16 SATURDAY

Moon Age Day 5 • Moon Sign Gemini

am ....

pm ....

You don't lack powers of attraction this weekend and Venus in the first is apt to put you in the path of the right sort of people. The good things in life start to come your way almost without you having to look and you could recognise the dawn of new romantic possibilities if you are an unattached Taurean.

17 SUNDAY

Moon Age Day 6 • Moon Sign Cancer

am ....

pm ....

An issue regarding a personal attachment at home could disturb your peace of mind this Sunday and it will be no time to sweep such a situation under the carpet. Loved ones can appear to be rather unfair or demanding and it might be worth looking at the situation carefully to see if there is someone around who is trying to get back at you for something that occurred in the past.

← NEGATIVE TREND						POSITIVE TREND →				
-5	-4	-3	-2	-1		+1	+2	+3	+4	+5
					LOVE					
					MONEY					
					LUCK					
					VITALITY					

18 MONDAY
Moon Age Day 7 • Moon Sign Cancer

am ....

pm ....

Check all travel arrangements carefully, as hold-ups or changes in plans seem likely. Wherever possible, be adaptable, though minor problems could still occur. On the whole this should prove to be a satisfactory start to the week, but you will need to exercise both self-discipline and patience if real headway is to be made.

19 TUESDAY
Moon Age Day 8 • Moon Sign Cancer

am ....

pm ....

The personal aspects of your world probably require a little shaking up, otherwise you could find yourself getting into an unnecessary and rather tedious rut. Your own aspirations are important, together with the like minded plans of those closest to you. Opinions of family members are likely to hold you back in some way.

20 WEDNESDAY
Moon Age Day 9 • Moon Sign Leo

am ....

pm ....

The Sun enters your solar first house in a new and extended period of vitality, in almost every sense of the word. Your personality is most impressive, patience is good and you find it generally simpler to attract the things you want from life. Professional schemes also prove to be highly favourable if you utilise them.

21 THURSDAY
Moon Age Day 10 • Moon Sign Leo

am ....

pm ....

You ought to find yourself pushed into the limelight to good effect today, which is probably the best day of the month for all leisure and entertainment aspects. Romantic matters also work to your advantage, though not everyone you come across has your own best interests at heart and so a little manoeuvering could prove to be necessary. Don't get mixed up with regard to responsibilities.

103

22 FRIDAY

Moon Age Day 11 • Moon Sign Virgo

am ....

pm ....

There is a square in your chart between Mercury and Neptune today so make sure you are fully aware of the finer points before committing yourself to any new business or professional project. Important deals are on offer, though you may need more time to consider them.

23 SATURDAY

Moon Age Day 12 • Moon Sign Virgo

am ....

pm ....

Despite the arrival of the weekend, this is a day of hard work, though beware of being in too much of a hurry to accomplish objectives immediately. Though minor challenges or personal confrontations could arise, these can be sidestepped with the right attitude. In any case, this is a productive time.

24 SUNDAY

Moon Age Day 13 • Moon Sign Libra

am ....

pm ....

Beware of appearing insincere in social gatherings or personal attachments. Meanwhile, those close to you could seem to agree whilst taking the contrary point of view in their own minds. The problem may be that you are fairly powerful at the moment, and that others find it difficult to affect your judgement either way. You need and can attract more credibility in the eyes of close friends.

←—NEGATIVE TREND						POSITIVE TREND —→				
-5	-4	-3	-2	-1		+1	+2	+3	+4	+5
					LOVE					
					MONEY					
					LUCK					
					VITALITY					

25 MONDAY

Moon Age Day 14 • Moon Sign Libra

am ....

pm ....

With a slight lull in physical energies brought about by the lunar low, the Sun in your sign may be inclined to tempt you to take on more than you can realistically handle. However, you have patience and determination, so that with effort even the position of the Moon is of relatively little importance to your overall success.

26 TUESDAY

Moon Age Day 15 • Moon Sign Scorpio

am ....

pm ....

With some slight dissatisfaction regarding personal affairs, you can be expecting too much of others and therefore could all to easily become intolerant of human failings generally. Taureans are sometimes accused of being possessive, and this is a trait that you could carry to extremes today unless you show extra special care.

27 WEDNESDAY

Moon Age Day 16 • Moon Sign Scorpio

am ....

pm ....

Intimate relationships have much to offer today and you can learn a great deal about yourself through the emotional ties that you have with others. Do be aware that you need to show some care when it comes to taking a leading role in the affairs of your partner as this could be seen as interference and rejected.

28 THURSDAY

Moon Age Day 17 • Moon Sign Sagittarius

am ....

pm ....

Though one-to-one relationships prove to be exciting and eventful, interactions become possible between yourself and your partner that show an exaggerated quality and if possible too much concern. It is all too easy for others to over-react to what you have to say today, so ensure that the cool and rational side of your Taurean nature is on display.

29 FRIDAY
Moon Age Day 18 • Moon Sign Sagittarius

am ....

pm ....

This would be an excellent time to get away from it all through travel or leisure pursuits. Many of your plans or schemes are presently taking care of themselves, so make time to do something new and interesting. A purposeful approach to relationships would certainly be advantageous at present.

30 SATURDAY
Moon Age Day 19 • Moon Sign Capricorn

am ....

pm ....

An association of the Sun and Jupiter in your solar chart at present, stimulates a sense of true optimism, both in yourself and in those closest to you. If others tend to make social arrangements on your behalf, then why not go along for the ride? There is also some mixing between business and pleasure to be considered.

1 SUNDAY
Moon Age Day 20 • Moon Sign Capricorn

am ....

pm ....

Excitement regarding the strictly social side of your life now begins to predominate and although a calmer atmosphere develops in some spheres of your life, social interaction is extremely important. There may be time later in the day when you possibly see a need for some serious talking, but only to clear up current misunderstandings or past miscalculations on your part. A Sunday of confidence.

← *NEGATIVE TREND*								*POSITIVE TREND* →			
-5	-4	-3	-2	-1				+1	+2	+3	+4	+5
					LOVE							
					MONEY							
					LUCK							
					VITALITY							

1994

YOUR MONTH AT A GLANCE

The twelve numbered boxes represent the important areas in your life. The key to the numbers you will find beneath the panel. A Sun above the number indicates that opportunities are around. A Cloud below the number, that you should be a bit defensive. Nothing above or below and life will be pretty ordinary.

1	2	3	4	5	6	7	8	9	10	11	12

KEY

1 Strength of Personality
2 Personal Finance
3 Useful Information Gathering
4 Domestic Affairs
5 Pleasure & Romance
6 Effective Work & Health

7 One to One Relationships
8 Questioning, Thinking & Deciding
9 External Influences / Education
10 Career Aspirations
11 Teamwork Activities
12 Unconscious Impulses

MAY HIGHS AND LOWS

Here, I show how the rhythm of the Moon will affect you this month. Like the tide, your energies and abilities will rise and fall with its pattern. When it is above the date line, go-for-it. When it is below the line you should be resting.

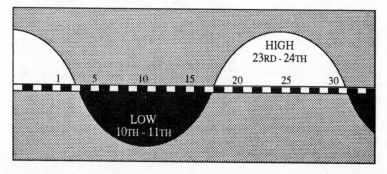

2 MONDAY
Moon Age Day 21 • Moon Sign Aquarius

am ....

pm ....

Beware of extravagent tendencies at the start of this week. Despite the present generosity you show to friends and loved ones, you ought to be counting the cost of life and perhaps drawing in your horns a little. Those close to you can have some surprises, particularly later in the day and this should at least put you in a happy frame of mind.

3 TUESDAY
Moon Age Day 22 • Moon Sign Aquarius

am ....

pm ....

Others seem to be pushing their weight around, particularly at work and in professional situations generally. It might be best to keep quiet and avoid conflicts which can get out of hand at present. In any case you would not want to be on the losing side of any argument.

4 WEDNESDAY
Moon Age Day 23 • Moon Sign Aquarius

am ....

pm ....

A conflict between Venus and Saturn could bring a period of minor financial set-backs and even losses if you are not careful to protect your own interests. In any situation it would be best to keep to tried and tested paths, and to plan ahead as carefully as you can. Leave gambling, or indeed any form of speculation until a later date.

5 THURSDAY
Moon Age Day 24 • Moon Sign Pisces

am ....

pm ....

It is so easy to make a big impression on others today that you barely have to try. Yours is perhaps the most popular sign of the zodiac at present, and you can benefit from this situation by being in the right place at the right time. Those closest to you and particularly good friends rely heavily on your support and approval at present.

6 FRIDAY
Moon Age Day 25 • Moon Sign Pisces

am ....

pm ....

The optimistic frame of mind you find yourself in is maintained today, particularly since heart-warming news, possibly from far away, will be coming to your doorstep now. This, together with other happenings puts you in a good mood for the remainder of the day. Social talks and discussions will stimulate your grey matter.

7 SATURDAY
Moon Age Day 26 • Moon Sign Aries

am ....

pm ....

You seem very motivated by service and by doing what you can for other people today, yet surprisingly you are not in a particularly self-sacrificing mood. Strong intuitions come and go and need to be listened to carefully. Life generally is made easier as you begin to create rewards for yourself, almost without trying.

8 SUNDAY
Moon Age Day 27 • Moon Sign Aries

am ....

pm ....

Unexpected points of disagreement are more or less inevitable today and particularly so in a personal relationship sense. Although you are quite willing to debate all situations, others are not so sensible or so logical at present. The one thing that you won't be willing to tolerate at the moment is any form of emotional blackmail.

← NEGATIVE TREND   *POSITIVE TREND →*

-5	-4	-3	-2	-1		+1	+2	+3	+4	+5
					LOVE	▒	▒			
					MONEY	▒	▒			
			▒		LUCK	▒				
					VITALITY	▒				

109

9 MONDAY
Moon Age Day 28 • Moon Sign Aries

am ....

pm ....

You start the new working week with the lunar high, so you should be looking good, feeling fit, and adopting today's motto which is 'optimism is everything'. Partly because of the vibes you give out, you tend to get a good reception from almost everyone you meet. Don't be frightened to take advantage of your powers of persuasion.

10 TUESDAY
Moon Age Day 0 • Moon Sign Taurus

am ....

pm ....

What you learn today can be turned to your advantage. Your objectives are sensible, and the goals that you aim for are modest. Because you are in such a positive frame of mind, you not only achieve what you intend, but probably much more besides. Friends are apt to do unexpected favours.

11 WEDNESDAY
Moon Age Day 1 • Moon Sign Taurus

am ....

pm ....

You have some ideas today that can be seen as being both clever and creative. This is particularly the case with regard to attracting more money and towards getting the material things you want from life. You tend to take on a 'nothing ventured, nothing gained' attitude and money matters show sustained improvement.

12 THURSDAY
Moon Age Day 2 • Moon Sign Gemini

am ....

pm ....

With a slight lack of self-confidence regarding the way you approach others, particularly influential figures, most of your ideas about yourself need reframing due to an overactive imagination. The more cool and objective you manage to remain, the better life turns in your direction. Contradictions are more or less inevitable.

13 FRIDAY

Moon Age Day 3 • Moon Sign Gemini

am ....

pm ....

Who says Friday the 13th has to be unlucky! You can make significant progress today with personal desires and plans which have a financial implication. Venus is strong in your solar second house, so your nearest and dearest are out to encourage you all they can. The world at large allows you to please yourself, so do so.

14 SATURDAY

Moon Age Day 4 • Moon Sign Gemini

am ....

pm ....

Despite the arrival of the weekend, you have a hectic schedule to keep to - organising your time carefully and keeping appointments wherever possible. It would be all to easy to allow others and situations generally to side-track you from important priorities, especially with pleasantries which abound just at present.

15 SUNDAY

Moon Age Day 5 • Moon Sign Cancer

am ....

pm ....

Much physical energy can be dissipated today, thanks to a conflict between the planets Mars and Neptune. Pace yourself carefully and take on only one task at a time. It could feel as if you are living in another world, and as a result your imagination can play tricks on you so don't take this situation seriously.

← *NEGATIVE TREND*　　　　　*POSITIVE TREND* →

-5	-4	-3	-2	-1		+1	+2	+3	+4	+5
					LOVE					
					MONEY					
					LUCK					
					VITALITY					

16 MONDAY
Moon Age Day 6 • Moon Sign Cancer

am ....

pm ....

Surprise visitors, phone calls and messages come rolling in. The Moon is in your solar fourth house, so at least you find yourself in excellent company. Minor successes come along in a professional field, if you are prepared to gamble. A satisfactory and productive time seems to be evident, but are you taking enough notice of it!

17 TUESDAY
Moon Age Day 7 • Moon Sign Leo

am ....

pm ....

The attitude of colleagues or associates can broaden your understanding of the world at large and you should treat today as a potentially valuable learning experience. Long journeys of any sort would be particularly favourable, either in reality, or still in the planning stage.

18 WEDNESDAY
Moon Age Day 8 • Moon Sign Leo

am ....

pm ....

Conflict between what partners expect of you and what you want of yourself, are more or less inevitable now. Wherever possible you should try to achieve a happy medium. There is a financial consideration - be careful who you lend money to. Planetary indications are that you may not see it again for some time.

19 THURSDAY
Moon Age Day 9 • Moon Sign Virgo

am ....

pm ....

You probably feel the need today to spend some time on social or pleasurable pursuits of your own invention and this can cause some resentment coming from the direction of your partner or close friends. This forms a tricky situation and you must decide early how you are going to split your time. At work be a typical Taurean, as methodical and careful as you possibly can be.

20 FRIDAY
Moon Age Day 10 • Moon Sign Virgo

am ....

pm ....

The association between the Sun and Pluto in your chart now can go either way. That means there could be serious demands or a power struggle as a partner tries to dominate the proceedings, or alternatively that this is the role you take on yourself. In either case, you should sit down and talk things through.

21 SATURDAY
Moon Age Day 11 • Moon Sign Libra

am ....

pm ....

The Sun enters your solar second house and after a period of some uncertainty financially brings a new time of relative financial gains. Attracting money, both today and for the next week or two, is not difficult and your typical Taurean qualities shine out for the next month. One word of caution, do beware of over stubborn behaviour.

22 SUNDAY
Moon Age Day 12 • Moon Sign Libra

am ....

pm ....

An easy going and carefree approach to daily life is what you can expect from yourself now; you can bring out the most appealing qualities in others while you are at it. It is easy to find compliments to pass on to others and there are important meetings and talks which go mostly in your favour.

← *NEGATIVE TREND*   *POSITIVE TREND* →

-5	-4	-3	-2	-1		+1	+2	+3	+4	+5
					LOVE					
					MONEY					
					LUCK					
					VITALITY					

23 MONDAY
Moon Age Day 13 • Moon Sign Scorpio

am ....

pm ....

The Moon occupies your opposite sign, bringing along the lunar low, so beware of committing yourself to any scheme, project or idea that you might want to back out of at a later date. It is fair to suggest that you may be looking on the blacker side of life, and you need to avoid negative thinking.

24 TUESDAY
Moon Age Day 14 • Moon Sign Scorpio

am ....

pm ....

Don't be frightened to assume a low profile, if that is what it takes to make life go slowly, steadily and sensibly at present. Many Taureans will now be catching up on minor tasks from the past and sorting out unfinished business. Not a day for high-flying plans, especially since you show a tendency to run out of steam.

25 WEDNESDAY
Moon Age Day 15 • Moon Sign Sagittarius

am ....

pm ....

Problems at work can be unresolved, or tricky, with an association between Mercury and the planet Uranus causing problems in your chart at present. If in any situation you cannot take corrective action yet, be patient. Do not allow the pressures of the material world to get you down. Some positive thinking would not go amiss.

26 THURSDAY
Moon Age Day 16 • Moon Sign Sagittarius

am ....

pm ....

Those closest to you can be over-sensitive to your remarks. However, since your general view of the world is improving you should not allow this to get you down. You remain essentially in a cheerful frame of mind and though you are careful not to take others for granted, you can trust your own judgement and should move forward in life as you really please.

27 FRIDAY   *Moon Age Day 17 • Moon Sign Capricorn*

am ....

pm ....

Your need for a change of scenery and for some variety in your life may go unfulfilled for the moment as unexpected demands are placed upon you. Even so, don't do any more for others than proves necessary and especially if the same people refuse to help themselves. A little selfishness could be necessary.

28 SATURDAY   *Moon Age Day 18 • Moon Sign Capricorn*

am ....

pm ....

The tempo of your everyday life is likely to quicken rapidly, though much of what happens around you is not only enjoyable, but also informative. Inspiring input comes from a host of different directions, not least of all your social life which really begins to take off. Family members have some interesting news.

29 SUNDAY   *Moon Age Day 19 • Moon Sign Capricorn*

am ....

pm ....

Involvements or discussions with others contribute towards a greater feeling of personal freedom and success. See what hints or help you can pick up from the world around and also bear in mind that a change of tack at present could be necessary and might work wonders, particularly in practical matters.

← NEGATIVE TREND   *POSITIVE TREND →*

-5	-4	-3	-2	-1			+1	+2	+3	+4	+5
					LOVE						
					MONEY						
					LUCK						
					VITALITY						

30 MONDAY
Moon Age Day 20 • Moon Sign Aquqrius

am ....

pm ....

You will more or less have to get used to the fact at the beginning of this week that you are at the beck and call of other people, particularly colleagues who seem to be struggling at present. However, there is no real desire or need on your part to seek the approval of anyone else and you should avoid worrying too much.

31 TUESDAY
Moon Age Day 21 • Moon Sign Aquqrius

am ....

pm ....

Familiar friends, faces and places are what mean the most to you today. In fact you may be slightly suspicious of any newcomers into your life. Your loyalty to those you care about is remarkable, a fact that others note and bear in mind. Benefits result from services offered to others in the past and you are very consciencious.

1 WEDNESDAY
Moon Age Day 22 • Moon Sign Pisces

am ....

pm ....

A very positive association of the planets Mars and Jupiter mean that you experience the best of both world's regarding personal plans and schemes and what others are doing for you. Your protective instincts are strong, which means you will be backing your partner or friends in almost any situation.

2 THURSDAY
Moon Age Day 23 • Moon Sign Pisces

am ....

pm ....

Certain friendships, or issues associated with them, could be something of a let down today. If you feel that life is being a little unfair, this could cause you to point the finger of blame at colleagues or friends in an unjustifiable way. Not only will this fail to score any points in life for you, but you will only take yourself to task about the fact later.

116

3 FRIDAY

Moon Age Day 24 • Moon Sign Aries

am ....

pm ....

Friendship issues can be affected inevitably by a financial matter. It is unlikely that you will be accused of actually cheating other people, but there may be indications that you are suspected of double dealing in some way. If this is the case, you will really have to speak your mind. Your loyalty to friends is tested severely.

4 SATURDAY

Moon Age Day 25 • Moon Sign Aries

am ....

pm ....

Your need for privacy or solitude may be a disturbing factor in the minds of those who are closest to you, particularly since you have been so socially inclined recently. Be patient with the reactions that come from others and be aware that life may remind you of a social attitude that you may have forgotten about.

5 SUNDAY

Moon Age Day 26 • Moon Sign Aries

am ....

pm ....

The lunar high comes along again, bringing high spirits and much optimism. Self confidence is not lacking and you are able to pat yourself on the back as a result of successes from the recent past. A bright and sunny day from a social view-point and you have plenty of opportunity and energy to get things done.

← *NEGATIVE TREND*   *POSITIVE TREND* →

-5	-4	-3	-2	-1			+1	+2	+3	+4	+5
					LOVE						
					MONEY						
					LUCK						
					VITALITY						

117

1994

YOUR MONTH AT A GLANCE

The twelve numbered boxes represent the important areas in your life. The key to the numbers you will find beneath the panel. A Sun above the number indicates that opportunities are around. A Cloud below the number, that you should be a bit defensive. Nothing above or below and life will be pretty ordinary.

				☀		☀		☀			
1	2	3	4	5	6	7	8	9	10	11	12
	☁										☁

KEY

1 Strength of Personality
2 Personal Finance
3 Useful Information Gathering
4 Domestic Affairs
5 Pleasure & Romance
6 Effective Work & Health

7 One to One Relationships
8 Questioning, Thinking & Deciding
9 External Influences / Education
10 Career Aspirations
11 Teamwork Activities
12 Unconscious Impulses

JUNE HIGHS AND LOWS

Here, I show how the rhythm of the Moon will affect you this month. Like the tide, your energies and abilities will rise and fall with its pattern. When it is above the date line, go-for-it. When it is below the line you should be resting.

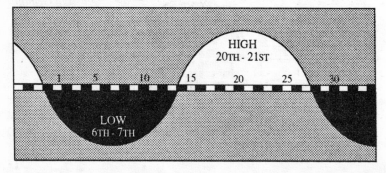

6 MONDAY
Moon Age Day 27 • Moon Sign Taurus

am ....

pm ....

Your get-up-and-go attitude does much to help personal matters move smoothly and easily today. Don't be afraid to ask favours from influential people as you may be surprised at the positive responses you are getting. Your love life can turn out to be more exciting than you think.

7 TUESDAY
Moon Age Day 28 • Moon Sign Taurus

am ....

pm ....

The retention of the lunar high in your chart today brings an emotional peak and loved ones especially are apt to make life very comfortable for you. Rewards come your way as the result of both present and past experiences and this would be the best time of the month to get new projects under way.

8 WEDNESDAY
Moon Age Day 29 • Moon Sign Gemini

am ....

pm ....

All social discussions, or important negotiations go smoothly as you are so much in touch with the thoughts and feelings of those close to you. Even usually awkward colleagues can be turned to your advantage with care, and your intuitions will tell you all you need to know about the world around you.

9 THURSDAY
Moon Age Day 0 • Moon Sign Gemini

am ....

pm ....

More give and take is now necessary, both in relationships and in associations of a more professional nature. For once you are certainly thinking too much about Number One and others will not fail to remind you of your duties and obligations if this proves to be the case. This is a period when finances can fluctuate wildly so spend or plan to spend with care.

10 FRIDAY
Moon Age Day 1 • Moon Sign Gemini

am ....

pm ....

There is news coming in today that can turn out to be a real eyebrow raiser. If this is regarding a mutual friend it will be best kept to yourself. Secrets are not hard to hold at present, even if there are certain individuals around who are trying to make you spill the beans. You can attend to a variety of interests simultaneously.

11 SATURDAY
Moon Age Day 2 • Moon Sign Cancer

am ....

pm ....

With Venus and the planet Uranus making an unusual combination in your chart at the moment, expect the unexpected and you won't go far wrong. Short journeys, meeting and appointments can all change at the last minute and though your best laid plans may be upset, what transpires can easily be turned to your advantage.

12 SUNDAY
Moon Age Day 3 • Moon Sign Cancer

am ....

pm ....

With a greater need than usual to experience the physical side of relationships, you are also very adventurous with regard to life as a whole. Feeling the need for hugs and kisses from those closest to you, reassurance is sought from every possible direction. Business deals or negotiations ought to be favourable.

← NEGATIVE TREND   POSITIVE TREND →

-5	-4	-3	-2	-1		+1	+2	+3	+4	+5
					LOVE					
					MONEY					
					LUCK					
					VITALITY					

120

13 MONDAY   *Moon Age Day 4 • Moon Sign Leo*

am ....

pm ....

Your mind is almost anywhere but on the task in hand, particularly regarding work plans or practical matters generally. It is easy to become bored with the hum-drum reality of life and the secret is to find something new and pleasant to distract you. Keep such considerations to the correct time and avoid being pushy.

14 TUESDAY   *Moon Age Day 5 • Moon Sign Leo*

am ....

pm ....

Family or domestic issues tend to be fairly troublesome and your partner may have thoughts on their mind which run contrary to your own opinions. Spending time out of doors or elsewhere seems to be something that inspires or cheers you at present, even so try to discover what others are thinking.

15 WEDNESDAY   *Moon Age Day 6 • Moon Sign Virgo*

am ....

pm ....

A new, though brief, period of domestic harmony is ushered in by the arrival of Venus into your solar fourth house. There may even be some reason for family celebrations at this time. Most spheres of your life go according to plan and great benefits can be gained through entertaining at home, or through relaxing with loved ones.

16 THURSDAY   *Moon Age Day 7 • Moon Sign Virgo*

am ....

pm ....

Some disagreements can now arise regarding money and the present association of the Sun and Pluto in your chart means that both sides in such situations will be fairly unwilling to back down. Although you should stand your ground in any potential conflict, don't stubbornly refuse to budge just for the sake of your own pride. Flexibility is all important.

121

17 FRIDAY

Moon Age Day 8 • Moon Sign Virgo

am ....

pm ....

Most obligations to others are carried out gladly and with high spirits. In fact most tasks tend to be a labour of love at present because you are being active and industrious. Personal or even professional involvements are also positively highlighted and this is generally a day for getting things done.

18 SATURDAY

Moon Age Day 9 • Moon Sign Libra

am ....

pm ....

Despite the arrival of Saturday, this is very much a business as usual sort of day. Working Taureans can make favourable progress, but even in this case you should not allow this to prevent you from considering new plans of a more social nature. Friends, or even your partner may rely upon you quite heavily.

19 SUNDAY

Moon Age Day 10 • Moon Sign Libra

am ....

pm ....

With the Moon in your opposite sign, everyday events go too slowly for your liking. However, if you can get out and about enjoy any summer weather that may be available and do your own thing, you may even fail to realise the slightly negative position of the Moon at present. Remaining cheerful proves to be all important.

← NEGATIVE TREND							POSITIVE TREND →				
-5	-4	-3	-2	-1			+1	+2	+3	+4	+5
					LOVE						
					MONEY						
					LUCK						
					VITALITY						

20 MONDAY
Moon Age Day 11 • Moon Sign Scorpio

am ....

pm ....

Avoid being hurried into making decisions that you are unsure of.
There is nothing to be gained from spur of the moment initiatives
and everything to win by being patient and allowing situations to
mature. Leave plenty of time in a day to day sense to recharge your
batteries before going back into action that would easily tire you.

21 TUESDAY
Moon Age Day 12 • Moon Sign Scorpio

am ....

pm ....

The Moon moves on and the Sun enters your solar third house,
bringing a boost to your general optimism and allowing you to
achieve your aims, merely by positive thinking and definite actions.
Self-confidence seems to abound and the advice that you give to
others can prove beneficial. Getting out and about is now a must.

22 WEDNESDAY
Moon Age Day 13 • Moon Sign Sagittarius

am ....

pm ....

You can now find yourself involved much more than usual in a
colleague's or friend's emotional problems. The private lives of
others become public as far as you are concerned and your assistance
is being counted on. You can certainly impart some of your age-old
wisdom today and it is well received.

23 THURSDAY
Moon Age Day 14 • Moon Sign Sagittarius

am ....

pm ....

Sympathies are aroused for your loved one and it seems you have
done little but help others for the last day or two. Despite your
generous heart you may be suffering from emotional fatigue and will
need to recuperate a little. Looking at your own life you should find
that things are running fairly smoothly and it is only accumulated
stress that can get you down right now.

24 FRIDAY
Moon Age Day 15 • Moon Sign Capricorn

am ....

pm ....

Those Taureans who have chosen this period to be on holiday are the luckiest of all. There is extra reason to feel excited today, whether you are on vacation or not. Attractive and entertaining people abound, even strangers and they will affect your view of life. Whatever you are doing today should be eventful.

25 SATURDAY
Moon Age Day 16 • Moon Sign Capricorn

am ....

pm ....

There may be heavy, although not altogether unexpected, domestic and family demands made upon you this weekend. Though you see these as serious responsibilities, do bear in mind that an all work and no play attitude is not to be advised at present. Even if you have to delay decisions until later, you need time to be yourself.

26 SUNDAY
Moon Age Day 17 • Moon Sign Aquarius

am ....

pm ....

Complicated issues arise at home with regard to all practical situations. However, if you choose your words skilfully, this is a situation that can easily be side-stepped. Out-witting others comes almost as second nature now and you need to be very subtle if any potential conflict brings you face to face with someone you know.

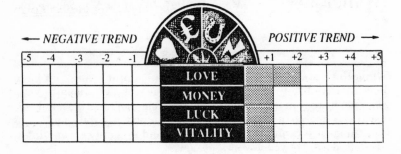

← NEGATIVE TREND							POSITIVE TREND →			
-5	-4	-3	-2	-1			+1	+2	+3	+4	+5
					LOVE						
					MONEY						
					LUCK						
					VITALITY						

27 MONDAY
Moon Age Day 18 • Moon Sign Aquarius

am ....

pm ....

You seem to show a strong desire to take the lead in relationships, you need also to beware of trying to take on too much responsibility for the sake of others. Get away from the mundane responsibilities of life as much as possible now, or the conscequences later may be more than you would wish.

28 TUESDAY
Moon Age Day 19 • Moon Sign Pisces

am ....

pm ....

The loyalty and trust that you have shown to someone close to you may prove to have been misplaced and this is certainly a day when others could let you down. However, there is no reason to disbelieve the world at large and any minor disappointments that do come along should be put to the back of your mind almost immediately.

29 WEDNESDAY
Moon Age Day 20 • Moon Sign Pisces

am ....

pm ....

You are now in a commanding position with regard to any important negotiations affecting your professional life. Others respect your ideas and opinions and may also supply you with the ability to plan journeys in the not too distant future. Even the shortest of outings can prove to be especially beneficial and surprises are abound.

30 THURSDAY
Moon Age Day 21 • Moon Sign Pisces

am ....

pm ....

Time spent alone, or perhaps with someone who is very dear to you is time well spent. Put serious obligations back in the cupboard when it proves possible to do so and don't be surprised if all practical matters appear to be a chore just now. Turning down social invitations is unavoidable, but will not cause problems if your motives for doing so were genuine.

125

1 FRIDAY

Moon Age Day 22 • Moon Sign Aries

am ....

pm ....

There are all sorts of people about who want to make rash promises, or who appear to be in a position to do you favours. Be careful! Self reliance is now the best way to accomplish your ideas, though in situations where you must be dependent on others, don't expect miracles. A confident attitude is important.

2 SATURDAY

Moon Age Day 23 • Moon Sign Aries

am ....

pm ....

It might be time to take a good look at your finances, particularly since there are elements that you have overlooked. At the same time, you are displaying some ingenious ideas to the world at large, and if these involve attracting money to yourself, then put them into action. All the same it wouldn't be advisable to tell people too much.

3 SUNDAY

Moon Age Day 24 • Moon Sign Taurus

am ....

pm ....

The Moon returns to your sign, so that energy and enthusiasm in abundance attend your life today. Put your best foot forward and press on with all current plans with the vigour that is so typical of your sign at the moment. Your ability to attract fortunate situations is certainly in operation right now.

← *NEGATIVE TREND*   *POSITIVE TREND* →

-5	-4	-3	-2	-1		+1	+2	+3	+4	+5
					LOVE					
					MONEY					
					LUCK					
					VITALITY					

1994

YOUR MONTH AT A GLANCE

The twelve numbered boxes represent the important areas in your life. The key to the numbers you will find beneath the panel. A Sun above the number indicates that opportunities are around. A Cloud below the number, that you should be a bit defensive. Nothing above or below and life will be pretty ordinary.

| 1 | 2 | 3 | 4 | 5 | 6 | 7 | 8 | 9 | 10 | 11 | 12 |

KEY

1 Strength of Personality
2 Personal Finance
3 Useful Information Gathering
4 Domestic Affairs
5 Pleasure & Romance
6 Effective Work & Health

7 One to One Relationships
8 Questioning, Thinking & Deciding
9 External Influences / Education
10 Career Aspirations
11 Teamwork Activities
12 Unconscious Impulses

JULY HIGHS AND LOWS

Here, I show how the rhythm of the Moon will affect you this month. Like the tide, your energies and abilities will rise and fall with its pattern. When it is above the date line, go-for-it. When it is below the line you should be resting.

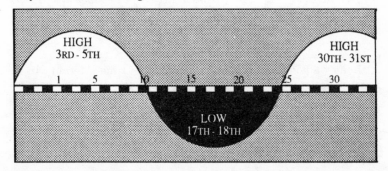

4 MONDAY
Moon Age Day 25 • Moon Sign Taurus

am ....

pm...

Since the week starts on the lunar high, you can expect a high profile today. Look forward to a warm reception and a happy atmosphere as far as your friends are concerned. Those closest to you are inclined to do unexpected things on your behalf, whilst personal plans and pet projects get an additional boost.

5 TUESDAY
Moon Age Day 26 • Moon Sign Taurus

am ....

pm...

You now tend to be more careful about how much money you are spending and on what. The Moon is in the second house and other planetary positions also indicate that your present frugality may also affect those closest to you. However, you shouldn't deny your partner the right to indulge themselves a little.

6 WEDNESDAY
Moon Age Day 27 • Moon Sign Gemini

am ....

pm ....

It looks as though the association of the Moon and the planet Uranus in your solar chart at present is inclined to make you rather more stubborn than would normally be the case even for Taurus. It seems as if others are deliberately setting themselves up against you, though the truth is that you are not viewing life fairly yourself.

7 THURSDAY
Moon Age Day 28 • Moon Sign Gemini

am ....

pm ....

Although a good and generally productive time, Mercury in the second house shows a tendency for you to over-work yourself physically. What you are doing is appreciated by others and particularly superiors, though loved ones may be less impressed and you will have to ask yourself if the effort is really worthwhile.

8 FRIDAY
Moon Age Day 0 • Moon Sign Cancer

am ....

pm ....

You are now happy in the company of others who in turn are pleased to have you around. You benefit from being on the same mental wavelength as colleagues and new ideas coming from your direction can find their support readily. Some confusion over deeper, more personal relationships, could reign as the day wears on.

9 SATURDAY
Moon Age Day 1 • Moon Sign Cancer

am ....

pm ....

It is house, home and family that captivate your imagination today with loved ones and perhaps especially your partner likely to encourage you to do just what pleases you. At the moment, you should take life easy and you certainly should not allow important practical or professional matters to get in the way of putting your feet up.

10 SUNDAY
Moon Age Day 2 • Moon Sign Leo

am ....

pm ....

Beware of making snap financial decisions, especially in a business sense. This is probably less than likely on a Sunday, though it is true to say that your desire nature in a number of directions is strongly stimulated at present. However, be careful of demanding more than your fair share of everything and avoid possessiveness.

← *NEGATIVE TREND*   *POSITIVE TREND* →

-5	-4	-3	-2	-1		+1	+2	+3	+4	+5
					LOVE					
					MONEY					
					LUCK					
					VITALITY					

11 MONDAY
Moon Age Day 3 • Moon Sign Leo

am ....

pm...

Little Mercury is now strong in your solar third house, making this an excellent time for travel, if only for the mental inspiration it provides. An impromptu journey might be good for this week, though those Taureans who have chosen this period for summer holidays may turn out to be the luckiest of all.

12 TUESDAY
Moon Age Day 4 • Moon Sign Leo

am ....

pm...

Out and about today, you can get a great deal from life simply by taking the chances that come your way. Most people should be fairly accommodating and are only too willing to allow a degree of self-choice. This may be slightly less true at home however, where some pressure could be coming your way.

13 WEDNESDAY
Moon Age Day 5 • Moon Sign Virgo

am ....

pm ....

All romantic pursuits and leisure involvements bring out your best side now. The Moon shows you to be particularly caring and attentive and significant love life developments can be expected around this time. Single Taureans should find new relationships blossoming and all Bulls can consider this to be an artistic interlude.

14 THURSDAY
Moon Age Day 6 • Moon Sign Virgo

am ....

pm ....

Though relationships seem to be going well enough, you could feel some slight dissatisfaction because you are over-emphasizing the glamour aspects of love and relationships. Of course, other people have their point of view, which it has to be said you may not be seeing as clearly at present as might normally be the case.

15 FRIDAY
Moon Age Day 7 • Moon Sign Libra

am ....

pm ....

A good day for progress at work or any important project for those Taureans who may not be working today. You can be subjected to sudden fits and starts, so try to be adaptable to any changes that occur. Where possible, work is best carried out alone, because in almost every respect you need to do things your own way.

16 SATURDAY
Moon Age Day 8 • Moon Sign Libra

am ....

pm ....

The lunar low of the month coincides with a Saturday, and so it is in the area of personal relationships that you tend to notice the Moon's presence in your life. What a partner or a friend has to say to you may prove to be a let down. However, don't try to force the issue or to change their mind. Chances are you would be wasting your time.

17 SUNDAY
Moon Age Day 9 • Moon Sign Scorpio

am ....

pm ....

Not really a very good time for taking on more commitments than you can realistically handle, despite the need that you feel at present to get ahead and to make progress in your life generally. Important decisions of any sort should be left until later, or at least until you get some expert assistance to guide you.

←— *NEGATIVE TREND*   *POSITIVE TREND* —→

	-5	-4	-3	-2	-1		+1	+2	+3	+4	+5
LOVE											
MONEY											
LUCK											
VITALITY											

18 MONDAY
Moon Age Day 10 • Moon Sign Scorpio

am ....

pm...

For the first part of the day at least, the lunar low is still around and so you won't start the working week with your physical energy level as high as you might wish. Leave future planning until later and attend to matters in the here and now. There is a stroke of luck in evidence, though it may affect your partner rather than yourself.

19 TUESDAY
Moon Age Day 11 • Moon Sign Sagittarius

am ....

pm...

It is possible that you could feel that you owe it to colleagues or friends to assist in their plans, or to perform some special favour on their behalf. Imagination is probably what leads the field here, though you cannot really lose out by giving someone a surprise in any case. You contribute to general happiness now.

20 WEDNESDAY
Moon Age Day 12 • Moon Sign Sagittarius

am ....

pm ....

Your attempts to press ahead with material plans and issues regarding money making can bring challenges into your life in one way or another. Even so, you are not about to be dejected by slight reversals and can push ahead regardless. Taurean persistence is extremely strong at present and woe betide any opposition.

21 THURSDAY
Moon Age Day 13 • Moon Sign Capricorn

am ....

pm ....

You should find yourself in a position to be out and about today, though if circumstances tie you to the spot, you must make time later on to do whatever takes your fancy. Whilst by and large this should be a fulfilling and interesting sort of day, beware of upsetting others in discussions simply on account of your tendency to be outspoken.

132

22 FRIDAY
Moon Age Day 14 • Moon Sign Capricorn

am ....

pm ....

With a strong association between Venus and Mars in your chart, the emphasis now should be on pleasure seeking. However, most Taureans are likely to go over the top at this time, due to the craving for luxury and physical comfort that is so strong at present. Even so, you are one of the most entertaining signs to be with now.

23 SATURDAY
Moon Age Day 15 • Moon Sign Aquarius

am ....

pm ....

Now the Sun enters your solar fourth house and puts the emphasis for the next month or so firmly upon your roots, home and family. Most of all you need to be around people who make you feel secure and wanted. This would include family members, old friends and of course your partner. It appears that family ties are paramount.

24 SUNDAY
Moon Age Day 16 • Moon Sign Aquarius

am ....

pm ....

A slightly less favourable trend today, with the Moon in your solar tenth house and jobs queueing up to wait for you. Remember, especially with this being Sunday, you are in charge of what is going on in your own life and you do not have to do things that go definitely against the grain.

← *NEGATIVE TREND*   *POSITIVE TREND* →

-5	-4	-3	-2	-1		+1	+2	+3	+4	+5
					LOVE					
					MONEY					
					LUCK					
					VITALITY					

25 MONDAY   *Moon Age Day 17 • Moon Sign Aquarius*

am ....

pm...

Although social pursuits and get-togethers offer the opportunity of much needed light relief, you could be brooding about something that has come from the direction of a friend, or a group member. The most advantageous situation would be to talk things through and to tell others how you feel about situations.

26 TUESDAY   *Moon Age Day 18 • Moon Sign Pisces*

am ....

pm...

With the slightly negative contact between Mercury and Mars in your solar chart now, you could be in a slightly indecisive state of mind, especially regarding important or professional arrangements. Certain options will not be open to you and final decisions have to be based upon the way the world is and not the way you wish it.

27 WEDNESDAY   *Moon Age Day 19 • Moon Sign Pisces*

am ....

pm ....

There is little doubt that a fairly low profile works best for you and indeed you may not even have the desire to deal with others to the extent that would normally be the case. Be especially careful with anyone who appears too good to be true as there is a distinct possibility that they are somehow deceptive.

28 THURSDAY   *Moon Age Day 20 • Moon Sign Aries*

am ....

pm ....

An eventful atmosphere is stimulated at home, by a contact in your solar chart between the Sun and planet Jupiter. Though this may not make for a particularly harmonious atmosphere, the agitation that comes from the direction of others does fund your own imagination and may encourage you to vent your own spleen about important issues.

29 FRIDAY
Moon Age Day 21 • Moon Sign Aries

am ....

pm ....

Do not be surprised if some of your ideas or opinions seem to be unusual or radical when viewed through the eyes of others. The reason is that you have a much wider angle of vision than the world at large at present, but even so try not to alienate those who have a more conservative view of life than you do at present.

30 SATURDAY
Moon Age Day 22 • Moon Sign Taurus

am ....

pm ....

The last weekend of the month sees the lunar high returning and forms the best time to put requests to those who are in a position to be of real help to your plans and schemes. The more you can get such people on your side the better. Many Taureans will also find themselves achieving a physical peak round about now.

31 SUNDAY
Moon Age Day 23 • Moon Sign Taurus

am ....

pm ....

Luck plays a large part in the running of the day. You could also be very captivated by the thought of freedom, the great outdoors, fresh fields and pastures new. It does appear that fate is trying to steer you in a more positive direction and you could do worse than listen to the little voice at the back of your mind that advises you.

← NEGATIVE TREND							POSITIVE TREND →				
-5	-4	-3	-2	-1			+1	+2	+3	+4	+5
					LOVE						
					MONEY						
					LUCK						
					VITALITY						

1994

YOUR MONTH AT A GLANCE

The twelve numbered boxes represent the important areas in your life. The key to the numbers you will find beneath the panel. A Sun above the number indicates that opportunities are around. A Cloud below the number, that you should be a bit defensive. Nothing above or below and life will be pretty ordinary.

1	2	3	4	5	6	7	8	9	10	11	12

KEY

1 Strength of Personality
2 Personal Finance
3 Useful Information Gathering
4 Domestic Affairs
5 Pleasure & Romance
6 Effective Work & Health
7 One to One Relationships
8 Questioning, Thinking & Deciding
9 External Influences / Education
10 Career Aspirations
11 Teamwork Activities
12 Unconscious Impulses

AUGUST HIGHS AND LOWS

Here, I show how the rhythm of the Moon will affect you this month. Like the tide, your energies and abilities will rise and fall with its pattern. When it is above the date line, go-for-it. When it is below the line you should be resting.

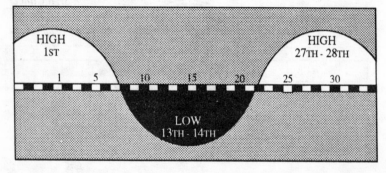

1 MONDAY
Moon Age Day 24 • Moon Sign Taurus

am ....

pm ....

Right from the start of the month, you are able to attract the kind of people into your life who prove to be not only interesting, but also useful. It is the social qualities of life that captivate your imagination and you appear to take life in an easy going way. However, your light touch with a loved one may be misinterpreted.

2 TUESDAY
Moon Age Day 25 • Moon Sign Gemini

am ....

pm ....

With the Moon in your solar second house, finances are apt to be a little unstable at this time. You are able to remain firm within the changes that affect your life now in a number of ways, and people in your vicinity give you the confidence to keep going. Don't shy away from a little speculation if you know that you will accumulate.

3 WEDNESDAY
Moon Age Day 26 • Moon Sign Gemini

am ....

pm ....

Fast, little Mercury is now entering your solar fourth house, bringing along a 'never a dull moment' period. Domestic situations are on your mind and your home life becomes a hive of activity. Do your best to join in all that is going on around you, it is unlikely that you will get much peace and quiet so try seek out some rest.

4 THURSDAY
Moon Age Day 27 • Moon Sign Cancer

am ....

pm ....

Minor headaches on the financial front could return and it is all too easy to realise at the moment where mistakes may have been made in the past. One thing that you do come to realise is that you may have been expecting rewards, without putting the necessary effort in. A situation that can easily be rectified now.

5 FRIDAY

Moon Age Day 28 • Moon Sign Cancer

am ....

pm ....

On what turns out to be an easy going and generally carefree sort of day, life jogs along under it's own momentum. Renewed confidence comes along to plan ahead and you are unlikely to miss any opportunity to do so. A friendly get-together later in the day works wonders and brings unconventional rewards.

6 SATURDAY

Moon Age Day 29 • Moon Sign Cancer

am ....

pm ....

Making improvements or changes around the homestead leads to an interesting weekend and some significant family developments. With the Moon in your solar fourth house, you do not need to look very much further than your own doorstep to find the contentment and fulfilment that you are seeking.

7 SUNDAY

Moon Age Day 0 • Moon Sign Leo

am ....

pm ....

Outside of the home today, social involvements improve and groups or associations of people seem to be much more agreeable than of late. Where you are in a position to go ahead with your own plans or schemes, a more ambitious and persevering individual begins to emerge and this really does tend to work wonders.

← *NEGATIVE TREND*   *POSITIVE TREND* →

-5	-4	-3	-2	-1			+1	+2	+3	+4	+5
					LOVE		▓				
					MONEY			▓			
			▓		LUCK						
					VITALITY		▓				

8 MONDAY
Moon Age Day 1 • Moon Sign Leo

am ....

pm ....

Remember at the start of this working week that not everyone is going to be as satisfied as you are by either the effort that you put in, or by what life tends to offer of it's own volition. Your own level of enthusiasm is very high, but the failure of others to respond could prove to be problematic, so do make allowances.

9 TUESDAY
Moon Age Day 2 • Moon Sign Virgo

am ....

pm ....

Though there is little doubt that you are willing to work hard for what you get, unexpected obstacles crowd in on the path to progress. This is an ideal opportunity for your Taurean patience to be brought to the fore, together with the fact that the trick to success lies in knowing what works best for you and which method to utilise.

10 WEDNESDAY
Moon Age Day 3 • Moon Sign Virgo

am ....

pm ....

It doesn't matter how hard you try, you won't be able to please everyone today, though this is a fact that should show out more in social situations than in professional ones. Friends can seem to be at odds with each other, so don't expect any miracles from get-togethers.

11 THURSDAY
Moon Age Day 4 • Moon Sign Libra

am ....

pm ....

Encouraging support, helpful input, or even invaluable assistance are all possible now. These not only have a bearing on your professional life, but also upon your personal plans. You can bounce ideas off others, particularly when working with colleagues and as a result should find yourself on the way to some very satisfying, if somewhat surprising results.

12 FRIDAY

Moon Age Day 5 • Moon Sign Libra

am ....

pm ....

As the working week draws to a close, you may want to make Friday mostly a family day, so that is where you receive most of your inspiration. People from the past tend to re-occur in your life and some of them could easily turn up unannounced. This isn't a bad time for reminiscing.

13 SATURDAY

Moon Age Day 6 • Moon Sign Scorpio

am ....

pm ....

Low energy and enthusiasm attends you as the Moon arrives at your opposite sign. Despite the arrival of the weekend, it is difficult to remain in a positive mood. Don't expect too many favours from the direction of other people, particularly since those you were counting on may be indisposed. Confrontations are certainly to be avoided.

14 SUNDAY

Moon Age Day 7 • Moon Sign Scorpio

am ....

pm ....

Still not exactly on top of the world, you get the best out of life by being out of the house and into the good fresh air, particularly if the weather turns out to be good. You can reverse the slightly negative attitudes of relatives or friends simply by being your usual understanding self.

← *NEGATIVE TREND*   *POSITIVE TREND* →

-5	-4	-3	-2	-1		+1	+2	+3	+4	+5
					LOVE					
					MONEY					
					LUCK					
					VITALITY					

15 MONDAY

Moon Age Day 8 • Moon Sign Sagittarius

am ....

pm ....

Though what you hear from intimates or close relatives sounds negative or even upsetting at times, at least you will be aware of the effect that you have been having on them and are more conversant with the way they are behaving. Don't be reluctant to hear the truth, either about friends, or even about yourself.

16 TUESDAY

Moon Age Day 9 • Moon Sign Sagittarius

am ....

pm ....

You have a strong need to assert your views at the present time, but be careful because others may not find you to be correct in your judgement and could also be a little shocked at your opinionated manner. There are good times to be had through interesting debates or discussions, though keep personal remarks to a minimum.

17 WEDNESDAY

Moon Age Day 10 • Moon Sign Sagittarius

am ....

pm ....

You really need to do what comes naturally today, with a slightly difficult association between the planets Venus and Saturn. You should not allow friends or associates to put a damper on your present plans; if you have to disregard the plans and opinions of others and go ahead yourself.

18 THURSDAY

Moon Age Day 11 • Moon Sign Capricorn

am ....

pm ....

Mercury, strong in your solar fifth house has an enlivening effect on love generally and romantic arrangements. Your present light and casual approach to life can win you admirers, but don't allow the attentions of outsiders to interfere with established relationships and the way that you view them. Continuity is important.

141

19 FRIDAY
Moon Age Day 12 • Moon Sign Capricorn

am ....

pm ....

Career pursuits, group schemes and all associations with others, may suffer from a tendency to become over-involved. It may be a case of too many cooks spoiling the broth, and where advice is concerned you should rely only on one or two people. In most situations it would be wise to back your own judgement.

20 SATURDAY
Moon Age Day 13 • Moon Sign Aquarius

am ....

pm ....

You need to be around things from your own past, which have a particular attachment for you at present. The desire to stick to your roots is very strong and if life projects you away from this feeling, you can feel out of sorts with yourself. Certainly this is an excellent day for contacting old friends or distant family members.

21 SUNDAY
Moon Age Day 14 • Moon Sign Aquarius

am ....

pm ....

Now you are much in demand socially, so make sure that you don't double book yourself as far as appointments are concerned. Keep to tried and trusted methods of doing things, as any sudden change of direction could easily lead to problems later in the day. Confidence may not be especially high.

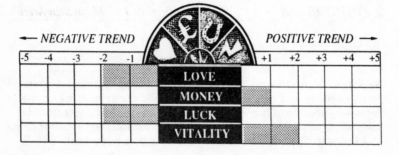

NEGATIVE TREND						POSITIVE TREND				
-5	-4	-3	-2	-1		+1	+2	+3	+4	+5
					LOVE					
					MONEY					
					LUCK					
					VITALITY					

22 MONDAY
Moon Age Day 15 • Moon Sign Pisces

am ....

pm ....

Look out now for a stroke of personal luck as Mercury makes a positive association with the planet Jupiter. The activities of a partner or a colleague help you to present a cheerful approach to the world and your personality shines out. This can be an inspiration to others if you allow it to be.

23 TUESDAY
Moon Age Day 16 • Moon Sign Pisces

am ....

pm ....

Now the Sun moves into your solar fifth house, heightening your sense of fulfilment through all romantic, leisure and creative pursuits. You can really be yourself now without feeling that you have to fit in as far as the world at large is concerned. Social conventions may be hard to fit in with, but artistic pursuits are well highlighted and need some extra effort.

24 WEDNESDAY
Moon Age Day 17 • Moon Sign Aries

am ....

pm ....

Most Taureans will be working behind the scenes today, carrying out the kind of tasks which have been left to one side for a while. Although you will do the best that you can to help and assist other people, there is a certain degree of self reliance around today and you need to follow your own course of action.

25 THURSDAY
Moon Age Day 18 • Moon Sign Aries

am ....

pm ....

The tempo of your everyday life quickens and any real fulfilment comes through busily pursuing your own objectives and personal goals. Be careful not to over-react to the very personal remarks that are being made by those close to you. Mentally you are very industrious and would work well on your own.

26 FRIDAY
Moon Age Day 19 • Moon Sign Aries

am ....

pm ....

With the lunar high comes a mental peak and you are able to see very clearly ahead towards your main objectives. There may not be too much opportunity for progress, but whatever does exist you tend to follow through to it's logical conclusions. Relationships can be very rewarding and today you can barely put a foot wrong.

27 SATURDAY
Moon Age Day 20 • Moon Sign Taurus

am ....

pm ....

If you are prepared to take the odd risk in important matters, the results may astonish you. Asking favours from others allows you to gain the kind of support which is extremely useful and even those people you don't know well are putting themselves in a position to be of assistance. You have the ability to talk to almost anyone.

28 SUNDAY
Moon Age Day 21 • Moon Sign Taurus

am ....

pm ....

It is still fairly easy to make smooth progress towards your own goals in life, though you may be unlikely to push situations along too quickly. A lucky element attends your life and this would be a reasonably good time for limited speculations of some sort.

← NEGATIVE TREND								POSITIVE TREND →		
-5	-4	-3	-2	-1		+1	+2	+3	+4	+5
					LOVE					
					MONEY					
					LUCK					
					VITALITY					

29 MONDAY
Moon Age Day 22 • Moon Sign Gemini

am ....

pm ....

Objectives are only achieved now through concentration and hard work. You find yourself at the start of the week, when achieving anything in terms of personal objectives can be a little difficult. However, finances should be showing significant improvement and you are capable of great achievement simply by plodding away.

30 TUESDAY
Moon Age Day 23 • Moon Sign Gemini

am ....

pm

It looks as though you are out to court popularity today due to the positive association of Mercury and Venus, so you can make a real impression. However, what you say and do can have a tinge of insincerity when viewed through the eyes of others so some care is necessary in this direction.

31 WEDNESDAY
Moon Age Day 24 • Moon Sign Gemini

am ....

pm ....

An ideal approach to life is one that is logical and practical at the moment. Today is excellent for all mental work and for problem solving. Even so, avoid becoming too narrow-minded in your attitude towards life as a whole, or you may find that rivals can easily get the better of you in debate or discussions of any kind.

1 THURSDAY
Moon Age Day 23 • Moon Sign Cancer

am ....

pm ....

Even your best laid plans can go awry today. Prepare yourself for meetings or appointments, but understand that they could end up being changed in some way. As long as you don't expect one hundred percent success for your efforts, all should go well. Even close friends may not be too reliable at present.

145

2 FRIDAY
Moon Age Day 26 • Moon Sign Cancer

am ....

pm ....

Serious issues are about regarding your love life. Listen very carefully to what your partner has to say and react accordingly, but only after due thought. You may not be able to enjoy yourself fully while such matters predominate but you should try to get change and diversity into your life wherever possible.

3 SATURDAY
Moon Age Day 27 • Moon Sign Leo

am ....

pm ....

Not everyone agrees with what you want to do today and while other people many be unlikely to stand in your way, they will make sure that their feelings are known. New career developments provide great encouragement, even if they are only in the planning stage this weekend. Leave time aside to socialise.

4 SUNDAY
Moon Age Day 28 • Moon Sign Leo

am ....

pm ....

Little Venus now enters your solar sixth house meaning that discussions and negotiations associated with practical or professional matters go extremely well, not only now but in the days ahead. Even though this is Sunday, you can pick up on some useful practical information which can be put to use later on.

← NEGATIVE TREND						POSITIVE TREND →				
-5	-4	-3	-2	-1		+1	+2	+3	+4	+5
					LOVE					
					MONEY					
					LUCK					
					VITALITY					

1994

YOUR MONTH AT A GLANCE

The twelve numbered boxes represent the important areas in your life. The key to the numbers you will find beneath the panel. A Sun above the number indicates that opportunities are around. A Cloud below the number, that you should be a bit defensive. Nothing above or below and life will be pretty ordinary.

| 1 | 2 | 3 | 4 | 5 | 6 | 7 | 8 | 9 | 10 | 11 | 12 |

KEY

1 Strength of Personality
2 Personal Finance
3 Useful Information Gathering
4 Domestic Affairs
5 Pleasure & Romance
6 Effective Work & Health

7 One to One Relationships
8 Questioning, Thinking & Deciding
9 External Influences / Education
10 Career Aspirations
11 Teamwork Activities
12 Unconscious Impulses

SEPTEMBER HIGHS AND LOWS

Here, I show how the rhythm of the Moon will affect you this month. Like the tide, your energies and abilities will rise and fall with its pattern. When it is above the date line, go-for-it. When it is below the line you should be resting.

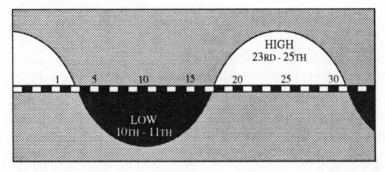

5 MONDAY
Moon Age Day 0 • Moon Sign Virgo

am ....

pm ....

It is in the direction of leisure activities that you tend to be turning today to achieve the best results of all. You are particularly happy to enjoy the company of familiar people and can probably be yourself more in company now than would often be the case. There is perhaps more of a desire to stay away from unknown situations.

6 TUESDAY
Moon Age Day 1 • Moon Sign Virgo

am ....

pm ....

Although you may not accomplish quite as much today as you would wish, this is really as a result of your present easy going attitude. For once you are weighing up too many options and need to realise that having made up your mind you should to stick to it. Advice from others is more or less useless at present.

7 WEDNESDAY
Moon Age Day 2 • Moon Sign Libra

am ....

pm ....

Intimate relationships are now definitely assisted by the entry of Venus into your solar seventh house. This infers a warm and harmonious interlude and one during which your powers of attraction are high. Those Taureans on the look out for a new relationship should find more success now with just a little effort.

8 THURSDAY
Moon Age Day 3 • Moon Sign Libra

am ....

pm ....

You should not expect work or career plans to follow tried and tested paths, whilst minor mishaps and the odd setback dogs your path. Where corrective action needs taking, be swift and don't hesitate to make things work out the way that you think is best. Confusion is almost inevitable probably from the direction of family members.

9 FRIDAY
Moon Age Day 4 • Moon Sign Libra

am ....

pm ....

The Moon moves into it's low position as far as you are concerned and this time round stimulates your emotional dependency on others. This is very definitely a good day to surround yourself with known friends and loved ones if possible. You can feel lonely quite easily, and certainly should not pursue independent projects.

10 SATURDAY
Moon Age Day 5 • Moon Sign Scorpio

am ....

pm ....

With the weekend, and the Moon still in its opposite position, you need to make plenty of time for rest and keep important matters at an even pace. There will be little gained by hurrying today and you need to work against a slight tendency towards pessimism. However, your partner should be reassuring.

11 SUNDAY
Moon Age Day 6 • Moon Sign Scorpio

am ....

pm ....

Relationships at work have a high spirited, easy going atmosphere, and information you now acquire is put to good use. You can save time later on and should not be afraid to use your initiative at every turn. An association between Mercury and Jupiter makes the next few days potentially rewarding.

← *NEGATIVE TREND*   *POSITIVE TREND* →

-5	-4	-3	-2	-1		+1	+2	+3	+4	+5
					LOVE					
					MONEY					
					LUCK					
					VITALITY					

149

12 MONDAY
Moon Age Day 7 • Moon Sign Sagittarius

am ....

pm ....

Those closest to you, especially in a family relationship sense could need some very careful handling today. The fact is that they are not explaining themselves rationally, or sensibly, so it will be difficult to take their statements at face value. Avoid becoming alarmed at the moods generated by your partner.

13 TUESDAY
Moon Age Day 8 • Moon Sign Sagittarius

am ....

pm ....

Young and unattached Taureans especially should be careful today when cultivating the attentions of the opposite sex as you may get more than you bargained for. Your attraction to others knows no bounds at present, even though it may be difficult for you to understand why they are so willing to put you in the limelight.

14 WEDNESDAY
Moon Age Day 9 • Moon Sign Capricorn

am ....

pm ....

Though you do feel strongly about certain aspects of life, there is just a slight danger that you may say the wrong thing. Impetuosity is not a trait that is typified by your sign, but with the Moon in your solar ninth house, today may be an exception. The best approach to take would be one of listening and then reacting steadily.

15 THURSDAY
Moon Age Day 10 • Moon Sign Capricorn

am ....

pm ....

This should be an exciting and eventful day romantically and one during which almost anything could happen and probably will. Make certain that you are where the action is for you will be sorry to miss it. A pleasurable day and one on which most of your friends easily come round to your point of view.

16 FRIDAY
Moon Age Day 11 • Moon Sign Aquarius

am ....

pm ....

Some project that you are anxious to pursue in the outside world may be affected by family concerns. Alternatively, the situation could be the other way round and you might discover that the needs of the family come up against obstacles from outside. You balance the personal and professional elements of your life well today.

17 SATURDAY
Moon Age Day 12 • Moon Sign Aquarius

am ....

pm ....

Words of wisdom drift in, courtesy of an old and trusted friend; perhaps forcing you to realise how much emphasis you place on their opinions. Differentiating between this and the gossip that comes from the direction of busy-bodies is not at all hard, as long as you stop to think. Later in the day social issues may be less exciting.

18 SUNDAY
Moon Age Day 13 • Moon Sign Pisces

am ....

pm ....

For the days ahead you are excellent in creative or artistic work and can make a powerful impression on your romantic partner. As a result, this would be an ideal time for discussing the 'ins' and 'outs' of any relationship, but would not be a favourable time for taking an action that could inspire jealousy in others.

← NEGATIVE TREND							POSITIVE TREND →				
-5	-4	-3	-2	-1			+1	+2	+3	+4	+5
					LOVE						
					MONEY						
					LUCK						
					VITALITY						

19 MONDAY
Moon Age Day 14 • Moon Sign Pisces

am ....

pm ....

Socially at the start of this new working week, you find yourself much in demand, though you can be pulled in two directions trying on the one hand to concentrate on the practicalities of life, whilst at the same time struggling to keep up with the requirements of a busy time outside of work.

20 TUESDAY
Moon Age Day 15 • Moon Sign Pisces

am ....

pm ....

Many Taureans will feel like spending more time on their own now and if you are one of them it might be necessary to put off social invitations in order to achieve your objective. In fact a little solitude or privacy could turn out to be a good thing, particularly since you feel that new responsibilities are being forced upon you all the time.

21 WEDNESDAY
Moon Age Day 16 • Moon Sign Aries

am ....

pm ....

You may have to ask yourself 'Where's the fire ?' today, for there is no doubt that you are in too much of a hurry regarding what turns out to be important matters. Snap decisions are definitely out of the window for the moment, likewise manoeuvering in professional matters unless you are absolutely certain of your opinion.

22 THURSDAY
Moon Age Day 17 • Moon Sign Aries

am ....

pm ....

After a rather confusing period, the lunar high brings more certainty today and allows you to enlist help and support from others for all important projects. Certainly your luck should be in and so you can afford to take a chance or two. A strong intuitive hunch could lead you down an exciting path emotionally, or even professionally.

23 FRIDAY

Moon Age Day 18 • Moon Sign Taurus

am ....

pm ....

Most sons and daughters of Venus will be looking good and feeling fit under the influence of a favourable Moon today. Do your best to inspire others with the confidence that you exude and don't be surprised if you find yourself pushed to the forefront in social activities.

24 SATURDAY

Moon Age Day 19 • Moon Sign Taurus

am ....

pm ....

Despite the arrival of the weekend, those that are able to contribute to your own personal successes should be with you in all your endeavours now. You should not be reluctant to take advantage, or to seek help when necessary and as long as you are still willing to make your voice heard, some important ears are open.

25 SUNDAY

Moon Age Day 20 • Moon Sign Taurus

am ....

pm ....

Although less busy than yesterday, today offers tremendous incentives simply to mix with friends, or to have a chat with acquaintances. Such potentials bring out the best in you and you will find on the way that others are only too willing to seek your advice in personal issues affecting their own lives.

← *NEGATIVE TREND*   *POSITIVE TREND* →

-5	-4	-3	-2	-1			+1	+2	+3	+4	+5
						LOVE					
						MONEY					
						LUCK					
						VITALITY					

26 MONDAY
Moon Age Day 21 • Moon Sign Gemini

am ....

pm ....

Finances can present you with minor headaches, so protect your interests fiscally as much as is possible. On a more practical level, don't be afraid to try out new, creative ideas at work, as otherwise it will be all too easy to find yourself in a rut. Create space to be on your own on those occasions when it seems to be necessary.

27 TUESDAY
Moon Age Day 22 • Moon Sign Gemini

am ....

pm ....

Mercury now enters your solar seventh house and indicates that news you have been waiting for from a partner or friend should arrive today, helping you to look forward to social plans. You are able to organise debates or discussions in your vicinity and are likely to be planning events that will affect your near future.

28 WEDNESDAY
Moon Age Day 23 • Moon Sign Cancer

am ....

pm ....

With Mars now making a favourable contact with Jupiter in your solar seventh house, this is one of the best periods of the month for love life and relationships generally. If you keep your eyes open you should now see the start of new friendships and promises being made romantically. Your own actions are most important though.

29 THURSDAY
Moon Age Day 24 • Moon Sign Cancer

am ....

pm ....

As a slight contrast to yesterday, you are not in a mood for listening too much to what others have to say. The gossip of relatives or friends irritates you significantly, the more so because you tend to take things personally. It might be an idea to try and understand the feelings and views of others if conflicts are to arise.

30 FRIDAY
Moon Age Day 25 • Moon Sign Cancer

am ....

pm ....

Home is probably the best place to be today and outside of work, which is necessary, to find that you tend to concentrate on relations and friends that occupy your immediate physical vicinity. If you have to travel today, try to stay open minded about the possibilities. No bad luck attends travel, simply a desire for things known.

1 SATURDAY
Moon Age Day 26 • Moon Sign Leo

am ....

pm ....

Material plans and professional goals should be showing signs of success as the weekend opens. A little extra effort with home based projects would be no bad thing, and would help to bring matters to a conclusion. Certainly a good day for a shopping spree, or for some very limited financial speculation. With the Moon in your solar sixth house, there should be something of a physical peak.

2 SUNDAY
Moon Age Day 27 • Moon Sign Leo

am ....

pm ....

There may be a surprise concerning social invitations coming in, but whatever happens regarding your dealings with others, it will be pleasant and rewarding in some way today. New affairs that may have begun romantically in the recent past now show excellent signs of progress; whilst settled Taureans are inclined to put their feet up.

← NEGATIVE TREND   POSITIVE TREND →

-5	-4	-3	-2	-1			+1	+2	+3	+4	+5
					LOVE						
					MONEY						
					LUCK						
					VITALITY						

1994

YOUR MONTH AT A GLANCE

The twelve numbered boxes represent the important areas in your life. The key to the numbers you will find beneath the panel. A Sun above the number indicates that opportunities are around. A Cloud below the number, that you should be a bit defensive. Nothing above or below and life will be pretty ordinary.

1	2	3	4	5	6	7	8	9	10	11	12

KEY

1 Strength of Personality	7 One to One Relationships
2 Personal Finance	8 Questioning, Thinking & Deciding
3 Useful Information Gathering	9 External Influences / Education
4 Domestic Affairs	10 Career Aspirations
5 Pleasure & Romance	11 Teamwork Activities
6 Effective Work & Health	12 Unconscious Impulses

OCTOBER HIGHS AND LOWS

Here, I show how the rhythm of the Moon will affect you this month. Like the tide, your energies and abilities will rise and fall with its pattern. When it is above the date line, go-for-it. When it is below the line you should be resting.

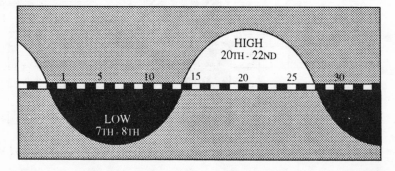

3 MONDAY
Moon Age Day 28 • Moon Sign Virgo

am ....

pm ....

Trying to balance the various requirements of your professional and personal life could be rather awkward at first. However, in a practical sense, help comes from the direction of colleagues who should encourage you to do what comes naturally. Once the pressures of work are over, confidence rises.

4 TUESDAY
Moon Age Day 29 • Moon Sign Virgo

am ....

pm ....

Changes can be made around the home and there is a positive impetus to do so now as Mars enters your solar fourth house. This is a most definite and advantageous sphere of your life, though loved ones could be rather demanding and even a little over assertive. Still, there is much pleasure to be gained from your social life.

5 WEDNESDAY
Moon Age Day 0 • Moon Sign Libra

am ....

pm ....

Be content to fulfil your obligations towards others as, just at present there is less scope to pursue your personal ambitions. You are inclined at the moment to 'pass the buck', particularly at a time when mistakes are very likely. However at the end of the day you will accept your responsibilities.

6 THURSDAY
Moon Age Day 1 • Moon Sign Libra

am ....

pm ....

Along comes the lunar low and this time around, the first effect that you will notice is that routine trends easily bore you. You will have to be your own inspiration right now, finding interesting things to do and covering up a temporary lull in your life with a positive attitude and a determination to succeed even occasionally against the odds.

7 FRIDAY

Moon Age Day 2 • Moon Sign Scorpio

am ....

pm ....

Taking life at an even and steady pace is well advised now. Attend to the simpler, though less demanding tasks that surround you because you don't feel up to the mark to tackle either important or demanding issues. Take the time out to have a chat and do realise that you are in charge of all your own life situations ultimately.

8 SATURDAY

Moon Age Day 3 • Moon Sign Scorpio

am ....

pm ....

With the Moon now moving on into a more favourable position, you will be taking on a more active role in attending to the emotional requirements of colleagues or friends. Certainly you can offer advice, but do remember that you can't live the life of another for them. By the evening, ensure that a partner is not feeling left out.

9 SUNDAY

Moon Age Day 4 • Moon Sign Sagittarius

am ....

pm ....

Socially you could be spreading yourself a little thinly, and might stand a chance of losing one or two important contacts in the outside world as a result. Certain aspects of life could leave you feeling unfulfilled and though you need to ring the changes socially, you also need to concentrate in specific directions in order to achieve your potential.

← *NEGATIVE TREND*   *POSITIVE TREND* →

-5	-4	-3	-2	-1		+1	+2	+3	+4	+5
					LOVE					
					MONEY					
					LUCK					
					VITALITY					

10 MONDAY
Moon Age Day 5 • Moon Sign Sagittarius

am ....

pm ....

Not a good day to be critical of others, for with the Sun forming a rather difficult aspect to Saturn, any criticism is inclined to bounce back in your direction. Even on those occasions when you consider you are looking towards someone's best interests, it may not be seen that way by them. Routine work proves to be rather unsatisfying.

11 TUESDAY
Moon Age Day 6 • Moon Sign Capricorn

am ....

pm ....

There ought to be plenty of excitement about today; variety is evident in social occurrences and there is always the possibility that you will meet an attractive or interesting stranger at some stage. Don't expect too much too quickly from any new liaison, at the same time travel matters are a must and you need to get out and about.

12 WEDNESDAY
Moon Age Day 7 • Moon Sign Capricorn

am ....

pm ....

It is never a dull moment at home, so if you are expecting a little peace and quiet, think again. At some stage during the day, don't be reluctant to sit down and talk over emotional issues with your partner, or a loved one who could be desperately in need of your advice. Suggestions can be followed up to your distinct advantage.

13 THURSDAY
Moon Age Day 8 • Moon Sign Aquarius

am ....

pm ....

It will be all to easy today to take others for granted, and particularly the people you rely on the most. A confident attitude works well on a personal level, whilst those you mix with professionally can be rather critical of your attitudes. A shift in perspective may prove to be necessary.

14 FRIDAY
Moon Age Day 9 • Moon Sign Aquarius

am ....

pm ....

Others may be trying to lead you up the garden path today. Once again this is a situation that affects you regarding your work, since personal aspects are more settled. Until this influence clears, keep your mind on pressing ahead and try not to rely on colleagues too much. If you suspect deception, you should ask a second opinion.

15 SATURDAY
Moon Age Day 10 • Moon Sign Pisces

am ....

pm ....

The more the merrier in terms of activity is the key to contentment this weekend. On a social footing, there is plenty to keep you occupied and any form of team effort shows good co-operation, whilst get togethers with friends thrive in an atmosphere of harmony. There may not be much in the way of peace and quiet.

16 SUNDAY
Moon Age Day 11 • Moon Sign Pisces

am ....

pm ....

Sudden and unexpected disruptions come along. Take all important situations one step at a time and move slowly towards your desired objectives. Concentrating is not easy and so a low key, though enjoyable period, is what you should seek. It might be sensible to put off demanding tasks altogether is possible.

← *NEGATIVE TREND*								*POSITIVE TREND* →			
-5	-4	-3	-2	-1			+1	+2	+3	+4	+5
					LOVE						
					MONEY						
					LUCK						
					VITALITY						

17 MONDAY
Moon Age Day 12 • Moon Sign Pisces

am ....

pm ....

Your susceptibility to the influence of colleagues or superiors may not all go well for the most advantageous day. All you can really do is to back your own judgement in matters you see as being important and also to listen to your intuition which is particularly strong at present. Hunches tend to pay off.

18 TUESDAY
Moon Age Day 13 • Moon Sign Aries

am ....

pm ....

Venus is strong in your solar seventh house and this means that one to one relationships prove to be plain sailing. As this appears to be the case throughout most of the month, this is the sphere of your life which brings the greatest happiness. You feel protected and warm when around the people who love you the most.

19 WEDNESDAY
Moon Age Day 14 • Moon Sign Aries

am ....

pm ....

Little Mercury moves backwards into your solar sixth house, not a fortunate occurrence since it can bring set-backs in work or practical matters. A time to consider details carefully, no matter how small they may be, since this can save problems later. Information you may have been expecting may have to be sought out personally.

20 THURSDAY
Moon Age Day 15 • Moon Sign Taurus

am ....

pm ....

With just a little positive thinking, you can make excellent progress in almost any direction today. Your ingenuity at spotting opportunities is truly remarkable now. All that is really required for ultimate success is to put your best foot forward. Financial gains are quite likely.

21 FRIDAY
Moon Age Day 16 • Moon Sign Taurus

am ....

pm ....

What an excellent time this is for requesting favours from colleagues or employees. Most of your approaches receive a warm reception from almost everyone. With the Moon back in your own sign, speculative matters work well, especially in a financial sense. Casual conversations carry important messages.

22 SATURDAY
Moon Age Day 17 • Moon Sign Taurus

am ....

pm ....

Disagreements come along at work, regarding the way any particular job ought to be performed. If the weekend finds you at home, a greater degree of compromise is possible, since once again it is the personal elements of life that work best for you. Results can be obtained regarding changes in and around your home.

23 SUNDAY
Moon Age Day 18 • Moon Sign Gemini

am ....

pm ....

The Sun enters your solar seventh house and really proves to be helpful in one to one relationships, re-confirming the strength and support that has been apparent throughout the whole month, though there is now a tendency to feel slightly in awe of certain individuals. All that is really required is a mixture of patience and self-belief for a week or two.

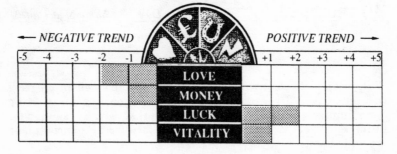

← NEGATIVE TREND								POSITIVE TREND →			
-5	-4	-3	-2	-1			+1	+2	+3	+4	+5
					LOVE						
					MONEY						
					LUCK						
					VITALITY						

24 MONDAY   *Moon Age Day 19 • Moon Sign Gemini*

am ....

pm ....

Very much a business as usual sort of day, with smooth and steady
progress and plenty of time for tying up loose ends. The one element
that could be missing from your life is a sense of fun which you will
really have to make for yourself. Others are not too co-operative.

25 TUESDAY   *Moon Age Day 20 • Moon Sign Cancer*

am ....

pm ....

Many of the surprises that come around now are of a fairly
complimentary nature, for with the positive aspect between Jupiter
and Neptune, your popularity is on the increase. Meanwhile a
partner, or perhaps a loved one may have unrealistic expectations of
you. If so, take time out to remind them that you are only human.

26 WEDNESDAY   *Moon Age Day 21 • Moon Sign Cancer*

am ....

pm ....

You ought now to be happily on the go and can easily handle several
different interests at once. Indecision surrounds you, but tends to
come from the direction of others and in the end you could even be
scratching your own head regarding the messes they tend to make.
Major decisions affecting home life should be put off for now.

27 THURSDAY   *Moon Age Day 22 • Moon Sign Cancer*

am ....

pm ....

An element of stress attends domestic or family matters as the
Moon comes under pressure from other planets whilst it now
occupies your solar fourth house. In most personal situations, it is
definitely a case of 'better the devil you know'. If you allow it,
minor disagreements can be blown up out of all proportion. Better
by far to realise the fact and restrain yourself.

28 FRIDAY
Moon Age Day 23 • Moon Sign Leo

am ....

pm ....

A day for considering business, particularly if you are a self
employed Taurean. You are fair in your dealings with other people,
which might be more than can be said for them, though you should
have the opportunity to get the better of rivals or competitors at
some stage during the day.

29 SATURDAY
Moon Age Day 24 • Moon Sign Leo

am ....

pm ....

News coming in from far away may be the source of false optimism
or hopes that are not really justified by circumstance. In almost any
situation wait until you know the details fully before making
relevant plans. You feel a need to be of service at present and look
towards other people to return the favour.

30 SUNDAY
Moon Age Day 25 • Moon Sign Virgo

am ....

pm ....

It's romantic and leisure activities that provide happy interludes in
your life now. Keeping an open mind, regarding important plans or
schemes that involve travel would be a good thing. New
opportunities are available if you choose to see them in the correct
light, but there are also compensations for the past mistakes you
want to live down.

← NEGATIVE TREND   *POSITIVE TREND →*

-5	-4	-3	-2	-1			+1	+2	+3	+4	+5
					LOVE						
					MONEY						
					LUCK						
					VITALITY						

31 MONDAY   *Moon Age Day 26 • Moon Sign Virgo*

am ....

pm ....

Though you can play the diplomat par excellence at the start of this
week, in all important social discussions a more forthright approach
would not go amiss, particularly at work. A tendency at present to
give in too easily may find you struggling under obligations that you
never intended to take on. .

1 TUESDAY   *Moon Age Day 27 • Moon Sign Libra*

am ....

pm ....

Input and co-operation from your partner in a personal sense, or
associates with regard to work, are both excellent. Even so, you are
in too much of a hurry to reach your objectives. Allowing yourself to
be highly strung today doesn't really help, so much so that there is
time to think and maybe even an hour to ignore routines altogether.

2 WEDNESDAY   *Moon Age Day 28 • Moon Sign Libra*

am ....

pm ....

Mercury forms a strange aspect with the planet Uranus indicating
that new ideas coming from the direction of colleagues could prove to
be truly inspirational. Some of them can form a key to open doors in
your own subconscious that have been locked for some time. Listen
in an make sure you maintain plenty of variety in your life.

3 THURSDAY   *Moon Age Day 0 • Moon Sign Scorpio*

am ....

pm ....

The lunar low indicates that physical energy will be somewhat
depleted and the answer is simple - don't give yourself too much to
do. Spend as much time with your nearest and dearest and when
you can find a moment or two, put your feet up and read a good book.
Not a time for moving mountains.

4 FRIDAY

Moon Age Day 1 • Moon Sign Scorpio

am ....

pm ....

Disappointments come along regarding personal matters, though only if you refuse to accept the possibility of them. Keep your expectations simple, otherwise you are likely to discover that it is just not your day. The most commonly accepted methods of doing things are by far the best ones to choose until tomorrow.

5 SATURDAY

Moon Age Day 2 • Moon Sign Sagittarius

am ....

pm ....

There is little doubt that the feeling of your partner, or perhaps a very close friend may surprise you in some way. For many Taureans, today could be a real eye opener. If you lean too heavily in an emotional sense on others, they in turn may move in the direction of greater freedom. Give and take is very important.

6 SUNDAY

Moon Age Day 3 • Moon Sign Sagittarius

am ....

pm ....

A good time for attracting the right kind of interesting individuals into your life. Now it is you who needs the freedom to pursue your own interests, so you won't be waiting around for the approval of anyone, no matter how close they may be to you. Make a determined effort to fill the cold winter months with new and different activities that friends may be willing to join in.

← *NEGATIVE TREND*   *POSITIVE TREND* →

-5	-4	-3	-2	-1			+1	+2	+3	+4	+5
					LOVE						
					MONEY						
					LUCK						
					VITALITY						

1994

YOUR MONTH AT A GLANCE

The twelve numbered boxes represent the important areas in your life. The key to the numbers you will find beneath the panel. A Sun above the number indicates that opportunities are around. A Cloud below the number, that you should be a bit defensive. Nothing above or below and life will be pretty ordinary.

							☀		☀		☀
1	2	3	4	5	6	7	8	9	10	11	12
		☁							☁		

KEY

1 Strength of Personality	7 One to One Relationships
2 Personal Finance	8 Questioning, Thinking & Deciding
3 Useful Information Gathering	9 External Influences / Education
4 Domestic Affairs	10 Career Aspirations
5 Pleasure & Romance	11 Teamwork Activities
6 Effective Work & Health	12 Unconscious Impulses

NOVEMBER HIGHS AND LOWS

Here, I show how the rhythm of the Moon will affect you this month. Like the tide, your energies and abilities will rise and fall with its pattern. When it is above the date line, go-for-it. When it is below the line you should be resting.

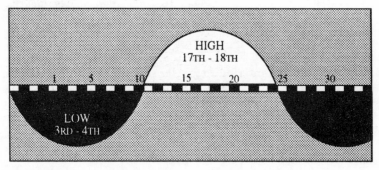

7 MONDAY

Moon Age Day 4 • Moon Sign Capricorn

am ....

pm ....

You ought to find opportunities now to broaden and expand your personal horizons. Some Taureans will feel they have been missing out on important projects recently and if you are one of them you can put the situation right. An optimistic day, and one on which you contribute to your ultimate success than has been possible lately.

8 TUESDAY

Moon Age Day 5 • Moon Sign Capricorn

am ....

pm ....

To others you appear to be stubborn today and it is true that the relative positions of Mercury and Pluto do not help the situation at all. In fact you are being firm and resolute and can quite easily turn situations in your desired direction. However, an obstinate view of relationships is rather unlikely to help.

9 WEDNESDAY

Moon Age Day 6 • Moon Sign Aquarius

am ....

pm ....

Career and professional matters bring challenging situations, continuing a week of some confrontation, but also increasing the ability you have to look after your own best interests. In most respects you will be ready for anything and others, if they are sensible, will be careful not to cross you.

10 THURSDAY

Moon Age Day 7 • Moon Sign Aquarius

am ....

pm ....

Little Mercury now entering your solar seventh house, stimulates a more reasonable and rational approach to personal relationships and to life in general. However, loved ones may misinterpret this as some coldness on your part. Since those closest to you know your true feelings at this time, any form of pretence would be a waste.

11 FRIDAY
Moon Age Day 8 • Moon Sign Aquarius

am ....

pm ....

Now you are truly back to a team spirit regarding co-operative ventures and the ability to make things happen in and around your home. The best work that you undertake today is on behalf of yourself, or at least in a situation where you can be in charge of others. Slight disappointments come from the direction of friends.

12 SATURDAY
Moon Age Day 9 • Moon Sign Pisces

am ....

pm ....

Some conflict is possible between the need for social input and the demands of loved ones and family members that are being made of you now. Those closest to you expect more than you are prepared to give and your priorities are placed elsewhere at present. Confidence is not exactly high, but the weekend does offer better potential.

13 SUNDAY
Moon Age Day 10 • Moon Sign Pisces

am ....

pm ....

Probably an excellent day for discussions within relationships and for setting matters straight where past misunderstandings are concerned. The present association of Mercury and Venus helps you to put your feelings into words and could also mean that positive responses are to be had from friends.

← NEGATIVE TREND   *POSITIVE TREND →*

-5	-4	-3	-2	-1		+1	+2	+3	+4	+5
					LOVE					
					MONEY					
					LUCK					
					VITALITY					

14 MONDAY
Moon Age Day 11 • Moon Sign Aries

am ....

pm ....

Feelings of personal reward come in as a new week gets underway.
This is mainly as a result of the help and support that you have
offered to others and on account of the people who are still drawing
from your strength. In fact you are so much in touch with the
requirements of those near you, forgetting yourself is all too easy.

15 TUESDAY
Moon Age Day 12 • Moon Sign Aries

am ....

pm ....

You benefit from spending time alone, locked into your own private
world, reflecting, unwinding, etc., while others need firmly
reminding of the fact that you have a life of your own if you are to
achieve any privacy. Work or new projects generally undertaken
behind the scenes go well and does not need too much support.

16 WEDNESDAY
Moon Age Day 13 • Moon Sign Aries

am ....

pm ....

With the lunar high now around, what an excellent time this would
be to make decisions regarding personal or professional schemes of
any sort. These should turn out to be lucky in some way, and you
may also discover how easy it is to get your own way with loved
ones. One or two relatives are still doing their best to be awkward.

17 THURSDAY
Moon Age Day 14 • Moon Sign Taurus

am ....

pm ....

You show the ability now to get ahead in most respects. Energy
levels are high and a fresh plan of action receives assistance from
unexpected quarters. General luck is apt to be on your side,
courtesy of the Moon, though this does not mean that you can get
away with skimping over details.

18 FRIDAY
Moon Age Day 15 • Moon Sign Taurus

am ....

pm ....

Even in those areas where apparent mishaps do occur, you should find later that these turn out to be a blessing in disguise. Physical and emotional levels achieve a peak, and most Taureans will feel that they can turn their hand to almost anything today.

19 SATURDAY
Moon Age Day 16 • Moon Sign Gemini

am ....

pm ....

Resist any domineering tendency in others, especially where work and financial commitments are concerned. You may have to get there under your own steam for a few days, as assistance from others is either unavailable or proves to be inadequate. Controversial subject matter in conversations should be avoided.

20 SUNDAY
Moon Age Day 17 • Moon Sign Gemini

am ....

pm ....

Loved ones, either in or out of the family have much to say for themselves and your remarks may just bring out the worst in them. Even so, there are situations that ought to be taken seriously and discussed, despite the fact that this is a potentially dangerous area. The only real problem is that you find it difficult to get a word in.

← *NEGATIVE TREND*   *POSITIVE TREND* →

-5	-4	-3	-2	-1		+1	+2	+3	+4	+5
					LOVE					
					MONEY					
					LUCK					
					VITALITY					

21 MONDAY
Moon Age Day 18 • Moon Sign Gemini

am ....

pm ....

This ought to be a generally productive day, where important talks and meetings are concerned. Don't expect too much excitement from a social side of your life however, particularly since those around you have plenty to say for themselves, some of which could be directed against you. Confirmation of one or two past suspicions can arise.

22 TUESDAY
Moon Age Day 19 • Moon Sign Cancer

am ....

pm ....

The Sun now enters your solar eighth house and despite the time of year brings a feeling of spring cleaning into your life when outmoded elements can be left behind once and for all. Certain plans and incentives need renovation, whilst intimate relationships benefit you through a new view of what is on offer.

23 WEDNESDAY
Moon Age Day 20 • Moon Sign Cancer

am ....

pm ....

Now embarking upon a more relaxing time, regarding everyday activities and objectives, short journeys perk you up and good news can come from relatively unexpected directions. Colleagues and loved ones are particularly supportive, but don't let partners do all the running or organising. You really need to pitch in yourself.

24 THURSDAY
Moon Age Day 21 • Moon Sign Leo

am ....

pm ....

There is a basic need now for a little more sparkle in your life and even romance could rear it's head as the working week jogs on. In a general sense, you should be feeling fairly fulfilled and it is the areas of travel, or one to one relationships that provide the best stimulus. An out of the ordinary attitude begins to dominate and shows how you can put spice into your life.

172

25 FRIDAY
Moon Age Day 22 • Moon Sign Leo

am ....

pm ....

Now you are taking an extra responsibility, either at work or at home, though what happens today may help you to clear up a backlog at work in order that you can clear the boards for future actions. Long term securities now seem important, though short term romantic encounters are certainly not out of the question.

26 SATURDAY
Moon Age Day 23 • Moon Sign Leo

am ....

pm ....

Although you are personally in a fairly easy going mood, the same cannot be said for your partner or a loved one. You may have to leave these people alone for a while, but they will come round in their own good time and it is clear that any attempt to reason with them at the moment probably won't work.

27 SUNDAY
Moon Age Day 24 • Moon Sign Virgo

am ....

pm ....

Unexpected financial demands come in, probably because they have been overlooked in the recent past. Money is likely to be in short supply, though you should be able to fulfil your obligations. Not a good day for putting things off, though an ideal time for social mixing and for seeking fresh fields and pastures new.

← NEGATIVE TREND   *POSITIVE TREND →*

-5	-4	-3	-2	-1		+1	+2	+3	+4	+5
					LOVE	▓				
					MONEY	▓	▓			
					LUCK	▓				
					VITALITY	▓	▓	▓		

28 MONDAY
Moon Age Day 25 • Moon Sign Virgo

am ....

pm ....

Something that you hear from a colleague or associate is almost certain to put a smile on your face and in fact good humour is the order of the day in all your dealings with the world at large. Your love life provides some pleasant experiences if you keep your eyes open for them. Too much reliance on others is not recommended.

29 TUESDAY
Moon Age Day 26 • Moon Sign Libra

am ....

pm ....

There really is the need for a change of tack, where work plans or future incentives are concerned. Try to think things over carefully before moving ahead, for although this is a significant period regarding long term objectives, you won't get anywhere by rushing your fences. In most routine jobs, slow and steady wins the race.

30 WEDNESDAY
Moon Age Day 27 • Moon Sign Libra

am ....

pm ....

Finishing the month on the lunar low, means that important decisions and activities may have to be shelved, whilst you get on and attend to the smaller issues of life. There is little doubt that the world tries to place more responsibility in your lap, though this is something you are inclined to turn away from just at the moment.

1 THURSDAY
Moon Age Day 28 • Moon Sign Scorpio

am ....

pm ....

As you start December, energy is still in fairly short supply. Keep your requirements of others simple and your demands to a minimum. This is certainly not the luckiest part of the month so remember, moderation in all things. You still cannot benefit from arguments of any sort, and a co-operative attitude wins friends.

2 FRIDAY
Moon Age Day 29 • Moon Sign Scorpio

am ....

pm ....

The Moon moves on, to be replaced by an association of Mercury and Venus. Today you may discover that your partner has overlooked certain practical or financial details that will need swift correction. You are firmly back in the driving seat and sorting out practical matters easily. Relationships by and large tend to be easy going,

3 SATURDAY
Moon Age Day 0 • Moon Sign Sagittarius

am ....

pm ....

Professional and personal progress may fail to live up to your expectations at first today, but remember this is the weekend; you may not be going anywhere in particular but you can make the most out of just taking time out to think. A slight problem is that you show a tendency to desire too much in the way of perfection.

4 SUNDAY
Moon Age Day 1 • Moon Sign Sagittarius

am ....

pm ....

Happy news comes in from far and wide relating to social arrangements. Take what opportunities you have for a change of scenery and light relief of some sort. Enjoy life on all levels while you can because there is some hard work ahead. For today, avoid anxiety and find somewhere peaceful to get a rest.

← *NEGATIVE TREND*   *POSITIVE TREND* →

-5	-4	-3	-2	-1			+1	+2	+3	+4	+5
					LOVE						
					MONEY						
					LUCK						
					VITALITY						

1994
YOUR MONTH AT A GLANCE

The twelve numbered boxes represent the important areas in your life. The key to the numbers you will find beneath the panel. A Sun above the number indicates that opportunities are around. A Cloud below the number, that you should be a bit defensive. Nothing above or below and life will be pretty ordinary.

1	2	3	4	5	6	7	8	9	10	11	12

KEY

1 Strength of Personality
2 Personal Finance
3 Useful Information Gathering
4 Domestic Affairs
5 Pleasure & Romance
6 Effective Work & Health

7 One to One Relationships
8 Questioning, Thinking & Deciding
9 External Influences / Education
10 Career Aspirations
11 Teamwork Activities
12 Unconscious Impulses

DECEMBER HIGHS AND LOWS

Here, I show how the rhythm of the Moon will affect you this month. Like the tide, your energies and abilities will rise and fall with its pattern. When it is above the date line, go-for-it. When it is below the line you should be resting.

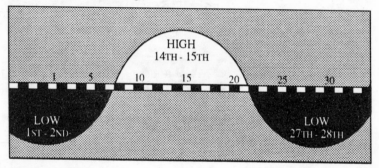

5 MONDAY
Moon Age Day 2 • Moon Sign Capricorn

am ....

pm ....

Getting things across to those people you work with could prove to be rather difficult today, if not impossible. Stubborn views seem to surround you and opinions are very fixed. Agreeing to disagree would appear to be the best course of action, plus a realisation that negotiations of almost any sort may have to be postponed,

6 TUESDAY
Moon Age Day 3 • Moon Sign Capricorn

am ....

pm ....

What looks like being a demanding day professionally stands before you and in fact this is true wherever progress has to be made. If little recognition or appreciation seems to be coming your way early on, at least important decisions made now should bring productive and very positive results later on.

7 WEDNESDAY
Moon Age Day 4 • Moon Sign Aquarius

am ....

pm ....

With the Sun strong in your solar eighth house you can feel a little insecure, mainly because you are aware of changes happening or signs of alterations to come in your personal life. The problem could be that you won't be sure where they are going to lead. You could do much worse than going with the flow.

8 THURSDAY
Moon Age Day 5 • Moon Sign Aquarius

am ....

pm ....

Although things should be stronger on a professional footing, the rigours of the last few days might indicate that you have cut yourself off a little emotionally from loved ones and friends. This is not a situation that is maintained for long, so don't take your own feelings on the subject too seriously.

9 FRIDAY

Moon Age Day 6 • Moon Sign Pisces

am ....

pm ....

With Jupiter now entering your solar eighth house, you could find today to be a turning point. Many of the events of the moment are clearing a path to future progress and even if this means saying goodbye to certain people, places or situations, ultimately there are benefits to be gained. Confusion tends to be removed.

10 SATURDAY

Moon Age Day 7 • Moon Sign Pisces

am ....

pm ....

With the weekend comes a boost to your social life and high spirits generally. You take any professional set-backs with a pinch of salt, but todays mishaps just may prove to be tomorrow's successes. Life at home should be smooth and relatively easy and confidence begins to grow.

11 SUNDAY

Moon Age Day 8 • Moon Sign Aries

am ....

pm ....

A brief lull in personal affairs allows you to recharge your batteries and probably to spend an hour or two on your own. If you find your-self without company altogether, don't take the situation too much to heart. There are plenty of social surprises in store further down the road.

← *NEGATIVE TREND*   *POSITIVE TREND* →

-5	-4	-3	-2	-1			+1	+2	+3	+4	+5
					LOVE						
					MONEY						
					LUCK						
					VITALITY						

12 MONDAY
Moon Age Day 9 • Moon Sign Aries

am ....

pm ....

Along comes a new period of excitement regarding pleasure activities and matters of the heart, courtesy of Mars entering your solar fifth house. Certainly you are very romantically inclined as the week opens and loved ones prove to be highly responsive. A caution though, you may be hogging the social limelight a little too much.

13 TUESDAY
Moon Age Day 10 • Moon Sign Aries

am ....

pm ....

The Moon moves back into your sign, bringing a day that should prove to be very fulfilling from a personal point of view, especially as you are already on a winning streak regarding career and personal objectives. Where you have new initiatives on your mind, you find it easy to get them off the ground.

14 WEDNESDAY
Moon Age Day 11 • Moon Sign Taurus

am ....

pm ....

There is a strong element of luck behind reactions and decisions at this time and the results speak for themselves. Good news is possible from a friend and the opportunity for a little self-congratulation comes along at some stage. You are especially anxious to please others at present.

15 THURSDAY
Moon Age Day 12 • Moon Sign Taurus

am ....

pm ....

Today marks the start of a physical peak. Get an early start in all important work matters and you will see how easy it is to make progress. An employee or a colleague may be in a position to perform some unexpected favours on your behalf. Don't procrastinate for Lady Luck is about.

16 FRIDAY
Moon Age Day 13 • Moon Sign Gemini

am ....

pm ....

As the working week draws to a close, it is important that you take care not to tread on the feelings of your partner or a loved one, as they may be feeling unusually sensitive. Although this is not as a result of your own actions, ill-considered movements on your part are not advisable.

17 SATURDAY
Moon Age Day 14 • Moon Sign Gemini

am ....

pm ....

Financial situations cause you to wonder if someone is trying to overpower ideas that are very important to you. The protagonist, if there is one, may be close to home. Certainly others could have different spending priorities right now, and joint money interests especially pose some problems.

18 SUNDAY
Moon Age Day 15 • Moon Sign Gemini

am ....

pm ....

Travel, meetings, appointments and social gatherings are all plain sailing. Life runs pretty much according to schedule and you can benefit from the practical advice of friends and relatives. Socially, you may need to lighten up, particularly as Christmas is just around the corner.

← NEGATIVE TREND   *POSITIVE TREND →*

-5	-4	-3	-2	-1			+1	+2	+3	+4	+5
					LOVE						
					MONEY						
					LUCK						
					VITALITY						

19 MONDAY
Moon Age Day 16 • Moon Sign Cancer

am ....

pm ....

Not a day to stand and stare. Mercury enters your solar ninth house and you are definitely on the go. Doing things for fun or on the spur of the moment will remind you that not everything has to be planned in detail. Opt for a change of scene whenever this is possible and keep away from regular daily activities that can be tedious.

20 TUESDAY
Moon Age Day 17 • Moon Sign Cancer

am ....

pm ....

Personal relationships can improve now, due to clearer powers of communication on your part. The ability to see things from your partner's point of view improves and you are probably becoming involved in the projects and interests of those closest to you. On a personal level, today should prove to be highly rewarding.

21 WEDNESDAY
Moon Age Day 18 • Moon Sign Leo

am ....

pm ....

The Sun enters your solar ninth house, bringing with it opportunities to broaden your mind and horizons generally. New personal or educational interests beckon and news, possibly coming from afar regarding social arrangements over the Christmas period, proves to be very stimulating if you listen with the right ear.

22 THURSDAY
Moon Age Day 19 • Moon Sign Leo

am ....

pm ....

It is one thing after another as far as your home life goes, but do be patient with family members and loved ones generally. It is true that demands being made by others are heavy, but you are more than usually content to attend to responsibilities and to cope with jobs one at a time.

23 FRIDAY

Moon Age Day 20 • Moon Sign Leo

am ....

pm ....

Romantic expectations are inclined to go unfulfilled today, but this may be due to requiring from others rather more than they are able or willing to give. If you are still at work today, professional and material plans are productive and this will be a good time to plan some kind of professional coup.

24 SATURDAY

Moon Age Day 21 • Moon Sign Virgo

am ....

pm ....

Anything but the usual routine is advisable today. An excellent time for something new or exciting and of course with Christmas only a day away, a period for getting together with others. A trip to a Theatre or Art Gallery might be especially stimulating.

25 SUNDAY

Moon Age Day 22 • Moon Sign Virgo

am ....

pm ....

Whether at home, or away for Christmas Day, you should prepare yourself for some pleasant surprises. This should be an excellent day all around, particularly if you adopt a come-what-may approach, rather than sticking to any kind of rigid schedule. You are in a family minded mood today which also helps.

26 MONDAY
Moon Age Day 23 • Moon Sign Libra

am ....

pm ....

With Christmas Day out of the way, you may be feeling especially lazy. The Moon occupies your solar sixth house and it isn't out of the question that family members accuse you of not pulling your weight. Nevertheless, in or near your home is probably a better place to be than out socialising right now.

27 TUESDAY
Moon Age Day 24 • Moon Sign Libra

am ....

pm ....

If surprising social invitations come along, it might be best to accept them now. In fact this could turn out to be the most exciting part of the Christmas Period in total, as friends and loved ones conspire to make life pleasurable for you. The day should prove to be very eventful.

28 WEDNESDAY
Moon Age Day 25 • Moon Sign Scorpio

am ....

pm ....

Things cool down a little as the lunar low comes along. Your spirits go into a slight decline and though personal relationships and get-togethers have a generally happy atmosphere, you may be feeling unable to join in the fun totally. A good period for spending just a little time alone.

29 THURSDAY
Moon Age Day 26 • Moon Sign Scorpio

am ....

pm ....

Some rather mundane chores to attend to today so try to get them finished as soon as possible. You could be easily bored by doing too much of the same thing, and can find yourself on the receiving end of let downs regarding a friend. Don't let such situations spoil your day and remain as active as possible.

30 FRIDAY
Moon Age Day 27 • Moon Sign Sagittarius

am ....

pm ....

Now the social animal in you comes to the fore, but beware of appearing insincere with others. From their point of view, it looks as though you are trying to score points in the popularity stakes and though you need to be tactful, it is important also that you are not afraid to say how you really feel.

31 SATURDAY
Moon Age Day 28 • Moon Sign Sagittarius

am ....

pm ....

Last minute organising is inevitable. Short term plans and schemes work well, so all in all a good time for New Year resolutions. You might be surprised at how energetic you feel, and there is significant opportunity to put your house in order before the commencement of the New Year. Look back and make a note of all your accomplishments.

← *NEGATIVE TREND*   *POSITIVE TREND* →

-5	-4	-3	-2	-1		+1	+2	+3	+4	+5
					LOVE					
					MONEY					
					LUCK					
					VITALITY					

RISING SIGNS
for TAURUS

Look along the top to find your date of birth, and down the side for
hour (or two) if appropriate for Summer Time.

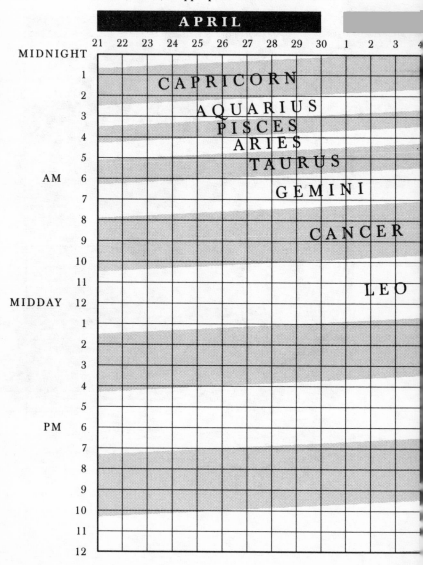

	APRIL												
	21	22	23	24	25	26	27	28	29	30	1	2	3	4

MIDNIGHT

1
2 — CAPRICORN
3 — AQUARIUS
4 — PISCES / ARIES
5 — TAURUS
AM 6
7 — GEMINI
8
9 — CANCER
10
11 — LEO
MIDDAY 12
1
2
3
4
5
PM 6
7
8
9
10
11
12

GMT birth time. Where they cross is your Rising Sign. Don't forget to subtract an

	6	7	8	9	10	11	12	13	14	15	16	17	18	19	20	21	

RGO

LIBRA

SCORPIO

SAGITTARIUS

THE ZODIAC AT A GLANCE

Placed	Sign	Symbol	Glyph	Polarity	Element	Quality	Planet	Glyph	Metal	Stone	Opposite
1	Aries	Ram	♈	+	Fire	Cardinal	Mars	♂	Iron	Bloodstone	Libra
2	Taurus	Bull	♉	–	Earth	Fixed	Venus	♀	Copper	Sapphire	Scorpio
3	Gemini	Twins	♊	+	Air	Mutable	Mercury	☿	Mercury	Tiger's Eye	Sagittarius
4	Cancer	Crab	♋	–	Water	Cardinal	Moon	☽	Silver	Pearl	Capricorn
5	Leo	Lion	♌	+	Fire	Fixed	Sun	☉	Gold	Ruby	Aquarius
6	Virgo	Maiden	♍	–	Earth	Mutable	Mercury	☿	Mercury	Sardonyx	Pisces
7	Libra	Scales	♎	+	Air	Cardinal	Venus	♀	Copper	Sapphire	Aries
8	Scorpio	Scorpion	♏	–	Water	Fixed	Pluto	♇	Plutonium	Jasper	Taurus
9	Sagittarius	Archer	♐	+	Fire	Mutable	Jupiter	♃	Tin	Topaz	Gemini
10	Capricorn	Goat	♑	–	Earth	Cardinal	Saturn	♄	Lead	Black Onyx	Cancer
11	Aquarius	Waterbearer	♒	+	Air	Fixed	Uranus	♅	Uranium	Amethyst	Leo
12	Pisces	Fishes	♓	–	Water	Mutable	Neptune	♆	Tin	Moonstone	Virgo

THE ZODIAC, PLANETS AND CORRESPONDENCES

In the first column of the table of correspondence, I list the signs of the Zodiac as they order themselves around their circle; starting with Aries and finishing with Pisces. In the last column, I list the signs as they will appear as opposites to those in the first column. For example, the sign which will be positioned opposite Aries, in a circular chart will be Libra.

Each sign of the Zodiac is either positive or negative. This by no means suggests that they are either 'good' or 'bad', but that they are either extrovert, outgoing, masculine signs (positive), or introspective, receptive, feminine signs (negative).

Each sign of the Zodiac will belong to one of the four Elements: Fire, Air, Earth or Water. Fire signs are creative and enthusiastic; Air signs are mentally active and thoughtful; Earth signs are constructive and practical; Water signs are emotional and have strong feelings.

Each sign of the Zodiac also belongs to one of the Qualities: Cardinal, Fixed or Mutable. Cardinal signs are initiators and pioneers; Fixed signs are consistent and inflexible; Mutable signs are educators and live to serve.

So, each sign will be either positive or negative, and will belong to one of the Elements and to one of the Qualities. You can see from the table, for example, that Aries is a positive, Cardinal, Fire sign.

The table also shows which planets rule each sign. For example, Mars is the ruling planet of Aries. Each planet represents a particular facet of personality - Mars represents physical energy and drive - and the sign which it rules is the one with which it has most in common,

The table also shows which metals and gem stones are associated with, or correspond with the signs of the Zodiac. Again, the correspondence is made when a metal or stone possesses properties that are held in common with a particular sign of the Zodiac. This system of correspondences can be extended to encompass any group, whether animal, vegetable or mineral - as well as people! For example, each sign of the Zodiac is associated with particular flowers and herbs, with particular animals, with particular towns and countries, and so on.

It is an interesting exercise when learning about astrology, to guess which sign of the Zodiac rules a particular thing, by trying to match its qualities with the appropriate sign.

The News of the Future

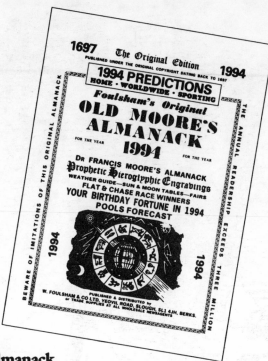

In the Almanack

Racing Tips — All the Classics. Dozens and dozens of lucky dates to follow — for Trainers and Jockeys.

Football and Greyhounds too.

Gardening Guide — Better Everything. Bigger; better; more colour. Whatever you want! Lunar planting is the key.

Fish Attack — Anglers get the upper hand and catch more fish. Dates, times and species to fish are all here.

With Key Zodiac Sign dates of course.

A great New Year investment for you.
An inexpensive, fun gift for your friends.

Look for it at W. H. Smith, John Menzies, Martins and all good newsagents.